Through the Hebrew Looking-Glass

Arab Stereotypes in Children's Literature

Fouzi El Asmar ,₁₄₃₇-

Amana Books
Vermont, USA

Zed Books Ltd.
London, UK

Through the Hebrew Looking Glass was first published
in 1986, by:

In the UK
Zed Books Ltd.
57 Caledonian Road
London N1 9BU

In the USA
Amana Books
58 Elliot Street
Brattleboro
Vermont 05301

Copyright © Fouzi El-Asmar, 1986.

Cover designed by Henry Iles.
Printed in the United Kingdom at The Bath Press, Avon.

British Library Cataloguing in Publication Data

el-Asmar, Fouzi
 Through the Hebrew looking glass : Arab
 stereotypes in children's literature.
 1. Children's literature, Hebrew — History and
 criticism   2. Politics and literature   3. Hebrew
 literature, Modern — 20th century
 I. Title
 892.4'6   PJ5021

 ISBN 0-86232-473-4
 ISBN 0-86232-474-2 Pbk

Library of Congress Catalog Card Number:

86-71359

ISBN 0-915597-39-X
ISBN 0-915597-37-3 Pbk

Contents

PJ
5021
.A8
1986

Foreword		vii
Acknowledgements		ix
Introduction		1
Historical and Political Context		2
Methodology		5
Significance of the Research		8
1.	**Zionist Political Thought before Herzl**	11
2.	**Political Zionism**	19
	A Country Empty of Population	20
	The Threat of Jewish Participation in the Socialist Revolutionary Movement	23
	The Defence of Western Interests in the Area	25
	Theodor Herzl	27
3.	**The Establishment of the State of Israel in 1948**	33
4.	**The Non-Existent Palestinian Arab**	51
5.	**Consciousness of the Conflict**	59
6.	**The Arab Character**	73
	Who Is the Arab?	73
	The Bedouins	80
	The Image of the Positive Arab	84
7.	**The Palestinian Arab Fighter and the Arab Soldier**	93
	Palestinian Fighters	93
	The Israeli 'Superman'	104
	The Arab Soldier	107
	The 1973 War	118
8.	**Conclusion**	123
	Bibliography	129
	Appendix	135

Contents

Foreword		vii
Acknowledgements		ix
Introduction		1
Historical and Political Context		2
Methodology		5
Significance of the Research		8
1.	**Zionist Political Thought before Herzl**	11
2.	**Political Zionism**	19
	A Country Empty of Population	20
	The Threat of Jewish Participation in the Socialist Revolutionary Movement	23
	The Defence of Western Interests in the Area	25
	Theodor Herzl	27
3.	**The Establishment of the State of Israel in 1948**	33
4.	**The Non-Existent Palestinian Arab**	51
5.	**Consciousness of the Conflict**	59
6.	**The Arab Character**	73
	Who Is the Arab?	73
	The Bedouins	80
	The Image of the Positive Arab	84
7.	**The Palestinian Arab Fighter and the Arab Soldier**	93
	Palestinian Fighters	93
	The Israeli 'Superman'	104
	The Arab Soldier	107
	The 1973 War	118
8.	**Conclusion**	123
	Bibliography	129
	Appendix	135

Foreword

This study can be divided into two main sections. Chapters 1 to 4 offer an introductory outline of Zionist thinking on the Palestinian Arab people prior to the establishment of the state of Israel in 1948, and of Israeli policies towards the remnant of the Palestinian Arab population which remained under Israeli rule. Chapters 5 to 8 constitute the main body of the study. They attempt to examine, through correlative content analysis, the image of the Palestinian Arab in Israeli Hebrew commercial story-books for children. Drawings and illustrations from the literature reviewed are reproduced in the appendix at the end of the study.

At the centre of the Middle East conflict lies the establishment of Israel as a Jewish state and the correlative dispossession of the mass of the Palestinian Arab people. Israeli policies are informed by the primary Zionist objective of securing the continued existence of Israel as a Jewish state and hence the continued exclusion of the Palestinian Arab from his/her homeland, Palestine. Such policies must generate, as indeed they have generated, continued conflict and recurrent wars.

In order to sustain a society willing to live in such conditions, it is necessary to educate the successive generations of Israeli Jewish youth to accept Zionist thought, and to accept the perpetual conflict with the Palestinian Arab people and the Arab world as a whole that Zionist and Israeli policies must generate.

This study examines the Zionist education offered to Israeli Jewish youth through commercial Hebrew children's literature as it is articulated in the image of the Arab in the literature reviewed.

It is the conclusion of the study that the literature reviewed aims to destroy any prospects for the young Israeli Jewish readership of achieving any understanding of the conflict that plays the paramount role in shaping their life and their destiny; and to destroy any prospect of regarding the Arab with a measure of understanding and respect; that it aims to perpetuate a lowly and despicable image of the Arab; and that in so doing it closely reflects mainstream Zionist thinking which, unable to reconcile itself to the

Palestinian Arab presence, aims to generate policies of separation and exclusion culminating in the policies of apartheid and occupation perpetrated by the state of Israel, as we know it today.

Acknowledgements

This thesis could never have been written and accomplished without the combined moral and economic help and the dedication of my professors, friends and wife. I am particularly grateful to Professor M.A. Shaban, Department of Arabic and Islamic Studies, University of Exeter, UK; Professor Adam Curle, School of Peace Studies, University of Bradford, UK; Dr Uri Davis, Research Fellow, Palestine Studies, Department of Arabic and Islamic Studies, University of Exeter, UK; the International Organization for the Elimination of All Forms of Racial Discrimination (EAFORD); the American Palestine Educational Foundation (APEF); Maria Teresa El-Asmar my wife, Robert Lebling Jr, and Ingrid A. Holland for the typing of the manuscript.

Introduction

The situation in the Middle East today is of major international significance. Many scholars and political thinkers would recognize unequivocally that the Israeli/Palestinian conflict lies at the root of the Middle East conflict, and that any attempt to achieve a long-lasting peaceful resolution of the conflict must be based on a just solution to what is conventionally termed the "Palestinian problem".

This study aims to offer a contribution to ongoing current research on the Israeli/Palestinian conflict. It will take as its point of departure an examination of the effects of the conflict as it has historically evolved on one aspect of Israeli Jewish culture, namely on the question of Zionist and Israeli education of Israeli Jewish youth as reflected in commercial story-books for children.

In this Introduction, I would like to point out that Zionist and Israeli education is responsible for fostering dangerous myths about Palestine, prevalent not only among Israeli Jewish youth, the direct subject of this study, but among the Jewish and non-Jewish general public. Among these are the myths of "a land without people for a people without land", "making the desert bloom", "the invincible Israeli army", "the Jewish mind", etc.

Education is a crucial issue in every society. It is a key institution for fostering a given culture and political identity able to secure continuity from generation to generation. Hence the importance of youth education both within and outside the formal framework of the school system. Initial research of some aspects of Israeli curricular and extra-curricular education has already been published (Adar and Adler 1965; Eppel 1972; Mar'i 1978; Lam; Peres *et al*). This study will be devoted to the examination of one aspect of Israeli extra-curricular education and culture, namely the image of the Palestinian Arab as presented in commercial Hebrew children's story-books published in Israel between 1948 and 1975 in the context of Zionist objectives, Israeli policies and the ensuing Israeli/Palestinian conflict.

1

Historical and Political Context

From the turn of the century, the Zionist movement (officially founded at the first Zionist Congress in Basle, 1897) increasingly came to predicate its efforts in Palestine on the achievement of two key objectives: 1) the establishment of a Jewish national home/Jewish state in Palestine, which could be successfully accomplished only at the expense of the native Palestinian Arab population; 2) the organization of mass Jewish immigration to Palestine in order to constitute a Jewish majority in a country populated largely by Palestinian Arabs.

In the context of the efforts of the Zionist movement to mobilize Western (Jewish and non-Jewish) public opinion in its support, it consistently promoted the myth of a "Palestine empty of population", inhabited at most by sparsely distributed nomad tribes who maintained no significant bond to the land. This constitutes a key element in the Zionist argument up to the present day. That this argument could be promoted (and accepted) in the face of the reality of Palestine with its major urban commercial centres of Jerusalem, Haifa, Acre, Lydda, Ramleh, Nablus, Hebron, etc., and the peasant hinterland which supported these centres and upon which they relied for their regular supply of staple foods, should give us a fair indication of the status of the native Palestinian in the Zionist and general Western mind.[1] We are reminded of Ahad ha-Am's warning, voiced in his major article written after his visit to Palestine in *Ha-Melitz* ("The Advocate") 24 Siven 1891, entitled "Truth from the Land of Israel":

> We abroad, are used to believing that the Land of Israel, is now almost totally desolate, a desert that is not sowed, and anyone who wishes to purchase these lands, may come and purchase as much as his heart desires. But in truth this is not the case. Throughout the country it is difficult to find fields that are not sowed; only sand fields and stone mountains that are not fit [to grow anything] but fruit trees, and this, also only after hard labour and great expense of clearing and reclamation — only these are not cultivated. (Ahad ha-Am 1965: 23)

Not surprisingly, the movement presented the Zionist cause in terms of carrying the beacon of Western light and culture into the barbaric backwaters of the Middle East, with the emphasis on seeking a legal charter in return for imperial services. For instance Ber Borochov, the founding ideologue of *Mapam*, the United Workers' Party, which printed on its banner "For Zionism, Socialism and Brotherhood among the Nations", wrote as follows:

> It is silly to suppose that some such [Empire] like England will withdraw on our behalf from one of its colonies just in order that it could with a clean conscience prohibit our immigration to the metropolis. This is just too high a price to pay for maintaining a clean conscience, unless this also involves some hope for expediency. And the expediency could be in respect to a number of aspects: the Jewish settlement, which will be under the protection of the Empire, will

constitute a convenient strategic base for the Empire in question for the purpose of defending other colonial territories from aggression by other states, or a cultural base, useful for the diffusion of the cultural and economic influence of the Empire among the savage native settlements in adjacent territories; our territory could be a new center for the production of raw materials for the metropolis . . .; we could create a new consumption market for the metropolis, and last — and that is the essential point — the Empire will establish with our help a new cultural-industrial focus into which it could divert its surplus capital. (Borochov 1954, 23)

The Zionist movement actively sought the imperial auspices of the German Kaiser, the Russian Tsar, the Ottoman Sultan, and finally the British Empire, which undertook to sponsor the Zionist effort in Palestine in terms of the Balfour Declaration of 2 November 1917.

Given this colonial context, the native population of Palestine could hardly be perceived by the Zionist movement as equally and fully human. The Zionist movement shared with other Western colonial efforts in the 18th and 19th centuries the White man's colonial burden.

Since the 1947 UN Partition Plan for Palestine, the country has suffered four major wars (the fifth war, namely the Lebanon war of 1982, falls outside the period of our research).

The war of 1948 (termed in Israel the War of Independence), the war of 1956, the Sinai Campaign (termed the Kadesh War), the war of 1967 (Six-Day War), and the 1973 war (Yom Kippur War), varied radically in their effects on the Israeli Jewish and Palestinian Arab societies. The 1948 war was the longest (May 1948 to January 1949), and caused the highest casualties. Yet on the other hand, the Jewish community in Palestine gained political independence and international recognition subsequent to this war. The status of the Arab society in those territories of Palestine which fell under Israeli sovereignty in consequence of the 1948 war changed radically. From an overwhelming majority it was transformed into a relatively small minority under Israeli Jewish rule. The 1956 war was carried out jointly with France and Britain in an attempt to reverse the nationalization of the Suez Canal by the Egyptian President, Gamal Abdul Nasser, and curb the rise of radical Arab nationalism, which was centred on the success of the 1952 young officers' coup against the monarchic regime of King Farouk in Egypt, and which raised explicitly the banner of anti-imperialism. The war resulted in a military victory for the Israeli army (Israeli troops reached the Suez Canal) on the one hand, and in a fatal political defeat for Israel on the other. Four months after announcing the establishment of the "Third Kingdom of Israel", Israel's Prime Minister Ben-Gurion was forced under a joint US-USSR ultimatum to pull the Israeli army back to the 1948 borders, and the French and the British were also forced to withdraw their troops from Egyptian soil.

In 1967, the Israeli victory over three Arab armies (Egypt, Jordan and Syria) resulted, or so it seemed until 1973, in unequivocal political successes, both in terms of territorial gains (three times as much as the territory of 1948 Israel), and in terms of establishing Israel (under American auspices) as a key regional power in the Middle East. The myth of the indefatigable Israeli army was firmly established, and Israeli Jewish society became euphoric. Against this background the 1973 war resulted in what was termed in Israel as "The Earthquake". The initially successful Arab surprise attack, the crushing of the Israeli frontline defences along the Suez Canal, the Gulf of Suez and the Golan Heights during the first days of the war, the unexpected length of the war (nine days), the fact that American supplies had to be airlifted from US bases directly to frontline airstrips in order to enable continued Israeli fighting, the relatively high level of casualties, the deterioration of Israel's international standing subsequent to the war, the increasing recognition in the West of the PLO (Palestine Liberation Organization) as the sole legitimate representative of the Palestinian people, and the international isolation of the state of Israel, have again determined a political climate very different from that prevailing in Israel before the war.

This study will undertake to examine what, if any, are the explicit and implicit effects of these (and other) contextual changes on the presentation of the Palestinian Arab in Israeli Hebrew commercial story-books for children published in Israel within the period 1948-75.

In order to understand the attitute of this literature towards Palestinian Arabs, we must examine the importance of Zionism as a dominant ideology.

The child in early formative years is influenced by a number of central agencies: parents and home, teachers and school, peers and environment. The literature that is read to children and the literature that they later learn to read, as well as communication in the mass media, all have a formative influence on child development. In other words, children invariably and inevitably are subject to formative influences from the adult world, and they are raised in a social context that can and does implicate them for life, determine their destiny, and consequently the destiny of their land, people and state. It is the adult world that determines whether the life of its children as individuals or as a generation will unfold in peace or under the shadow of continual war, in progress or in deprivation. On the other hand, children have no critical or direct influence on the adult world. This, however, does not preclude the possibility of the child developing a theory of its own on certain subjects. Clearly, however, such theories would reflect to a large extent the influence of adult society.

In the course of this study we shall therefore have to present the policies and the means utilized by the Zionist movement for the establishment of the Jewish state. We shall examine how these are treated by the authors of this literature and how they chose to present to the Jewish Hebrew-speaking youth in Israel the tragedy that has been inflicted upon the Palestinian Arab people who have lived in this part of the world for many generations.

In order to undertake such a study, it is necessary first to present an outline of the Zionist Palestinian conflict. It is in the framework of such an outline that the specific subject of our research can be adequately expounded.

Clearly it is beyond the capacity of an individual researcher to embrace all aspects of the field in question. This study will therefore be restricted to the examination of the image of the Palestinian Arab as presented to the Jewish (Hebrew-speaking) youth. The relevant empirical data could be categorized as follows: 1) commercial Hebrew children's story-books (children being defined as elementary-school-age youth, 6-14 years old); 2) elementary-school textbooks in literature, history and geography; 3) children's newspapers and magazines; 4) children's films.

This study will be confined to the examination of the image of the Palestinian Arab as presented in commercial Hebrew children's story-books alone.

Methodology

In 1976 I travelled to Israel in order to collect the primary source material for this study. As my first work of reference I used *The General Book Catalogue* (Steiner 1975) which lists all books (for adults and children) printed and published in Palestine and, following 1948, in Israel in Hebrew. The total list consists of 3,366 titles.

As a first measure of selection I eliminated from the list all books by non-Israeli authors, namely, books published in Hebrew translation (1,400 books; 40% of the titles). Throughout the following two months, I reviewed all the remaining titles in the public libraries of Lydda, Petah Tiqwah and Tel Aviv, and in the National Library at the Hebrew University in Jerusalem. I listed and subsequently purchased or photocopied every title dealing with the subject of the Arab. This collection I took with me back to the United Kingdom. It consists of 205 titles.[2]

The bibliography for this study clearly indicates that there is a group of authors who effectively dominate the field of commercial Israeli Hebrew children's literature that deals meaningfully with the question of the Arabs. These authors tend to publish series of children's books, and in some cases the same author publishes parallel series under pseudonyms.

Of the 205 books reviewed, 80 books (40%) were written by four authors: Abner Karmeli (35 titles); Yigal Mosinson (21 titles); On Sarig (17 titles); Haim Eliav (seven titles). In reality the monopoly is even more radical, since On Sarig is a pseudonym for Abner Karmeli. The remaining 125 titles (60%) were written by 60 different authors. This reality is reflected in the account of this research in that the number of authors quoted in the references is smaller than one would initially expect.

The concept of stereotyping is central to this research. The concept was first introduced into social science discourse in the 1940s (see *International Encyclopaedia of Social Science*, Vol. 15, p. 259).

The first definition of the term was by Walter Lippman. Lippman (1922) argues that the term "stereotype" offers a way of handling the real environment which is altogether too big, too complex and too fleeting for direct acquaintance.

Since the publication of Lippman's book, hundreds of articles and papers have been published on the question of stereotyping. By and large the main body of literature has demonstrated that: "Stereotypes are a key variable in any attempt to develop a general theory of prejudice" (Cauthen, Robinson and Krauss 1971: 120).

The literature offers various definitions for the concept of stereotype such as: ". . . stereotypes are a set of beliefs and disbeliefs, about any group of people . . ." (Ehrlich 1973: 20); ". . . a category that singles out an individual as sharing assumed characteristics on the basis of his group membership . . ." (Vander 1966: 80-1); "Stereotypes are essentially linguistic behaviours, which vary with social class and with nationality" (Cauthen, Robinson and Krauss 1971: 103).

Many researchers believe that there is always a grain of truth in the stereotype. The anthropologist Clyde Kluckhohn argues: "There is almost always a grain of truth in the vicious stereotypes that are created, and this helps us swallow the major portion of untruth, because we must in order to find a partial escape from confusion . . ." (Kluckhohn 1971: 138).

Of course there is always a grain of truth in the stereotype but it is necessary to exercise extreme caution in identifying this grain of truth and explicating its meaning in context. For example, Israel defeated the Arabs in three consecutive wars (1948, 1956, 1967). On the basis of this fact, the literature reviewed in this study developed the bloated stereotype of an Arab as a mentally retarded coward who is reluctant to fight, an informer, a pawn ignorant of the cause for which he is asked to fight, a soldier forced into battle under duress and coercion, and with similar stereotypical features which are blatantly false and obviously racist. But underpinning this distorted stereotype, there is an obvious grain of truth: the Arabs were defeated in three consecutive wars by the Israeli army.

It is important to note that the stereotype is used to serve political objectives and is subject to extreme changes and fluctuations related to changes and fluctuations in the relevant political context. Thus, the stereotype of the Japanese in the United States before the outbreak of World War II typically demonstrated such features as intelligence and wisdom. This stereotype, however, rapidly altered after the outbreak of the war, exhibiting such features as slyness as its central characteristic (see for example Cauthen, Robinson and Krauss 1971: 119). Needless to say, over the three decades after World War II the Japanese stereotype was reconstituted again to feature intelligence and wisdom as its central characteristics, obviously reflecting the post-war political situation.

A parallel process applied to the image of the Arab in Israeli Hebrew children's literature. Today, Israeli researchers can identify changes in the image of the Arab after the 1973 war. Thus, Professor Kalman Benjamin of the Hebrew University in Jerusalem reports that today the image of the Arab in the eyes of Israeli youth demonstrates more positive manly features. The Egyptian Arabs, for instance, are portrayed as quick, socially healthy, confident, manly and open to compromise, whereas in similar research carried out by Professor Kalman Benjamin shortly after the 1967 war, the image of the Arab in the eyes of Israeli youth demonstrated radically negative features: ugly, old, slow, weak and unsuccessful (*Yediot Aharonot*, 12 November 1980, and *Jewish Week*, 1-7 January 1981).

The stereotype of the Arab which is the subject of our research is the product of an ideological project, namely Zionism, which constituted a negative stereotype of the Arab and applied this stereotype to assist in the promotion of its overall political objectives. It will not be possible to assess this stereotype except in terms of its political-historical context.

Finally, the methodological tool for this research is phenomenological or qualitative content analysis.

Content analysis in its contemporary application was first used in the United States by students of journalism (and later by sociologists) to study the content of American newspapers. It was subsequently given an important stimulus through the work of Lasswell and his associates, and the growing interest in propaganda and public opinion (for example Lasswell *et al.* 1949).

During World War II content analysis was employed by government departments responsible for mass communication and foreign broadcasts. Following the war, content analysis was soon given commercial applications in various fields (analysis of editorial opinion, press intelligence, etc.).

In parallel, content analysis developed into a key methodological instrument in all branches of the social sciences and the humanities. As Berelson points out, it has been used to answer such diverse questions as:

How have the slogans of May Day propaganda in the USSR changed during the Soviet regime?
What are the dominant images in Shakespeare's plays?
How is the writer's personality structure reflected in what he writes?
How do the values in American plays differ from those in German plays of the same time? How do the values in Boy Scout literature in the United States differ from those in *Hitlerjugend* literature?
What are the major trends in the use of research literature by chemists and physicists since 1900?
How are minority ethnic groups treated in short stories in popular magazines?
How can communications suspected of subversion be tested for their "propaganda" component?
How do newspapers and radio compare in their treatment of a sensational murder case?
What makes writing readable?
In what ways do motion pictures reflect popular feelings and desires?
What are the similarities and differences in the political symbols which come to the attention of people in the major power states?

What happens to a "good book" when it is made into a movie?
What intelligence data can be secured from analysis of enemy propaganda?
(Berelson 1952: 13-14).

Qualitative content analysis is conventionally characterized as being relatively less concerned with content as such than with content as a "reflection" of "deeper" phenomena; utilizing more complex themes and employing less formalized categorization than quantitative analysis; and tending to focus on the intentions of the communicator and the effects of the communication upon the audience (Berelson 1952: 123-8; see also Mayntz, Holm and Hoebner 1976).

It is my hope that this study of the image of the Palestinian Arab in Israeli Hebrew commercial story-books for children will be considered a modest contribution to the body of academic literature resulting from the insight offered by qualitative content analysis.

Significance of the Research

As a Palestinian Arab and a citizen of the state of Israel, I believe that the two peoples, the Israeli Jewish and the Palestinian Arab, are fated to a common life and a common destiny; that a situation must be created where their futures will be complementary to each other rather than aiming at mutual destruction. Jews live and will continue to live in a predominantly Arab Mashreq. But the basis for a common future between the two peoples is yet to be created by Palestinian Arabs and Israeli Jews together. Such a basis cannot be constructed by the Zionist movement or a Zionist state of Israel. On the contrary, these are largely responsible for the history of antagonism and murderous conflict which has characterized life in Palestine during the past half-century.

Every effort must be made to create a new common basis founded on equality of human, political and national rights for both peoples. Both societies are in urgent need of a critical reassessment of their curricular and extra-curricular literature. It is only on the basis of such a critical reassessment that a historically viable alternative can be constructed. This study aims to make a partial contribution to this effort through the critical examination of commercial Israeli Hebrew children's story-books published in Israel between 1948 and 1975.

Notes

1. For an excellent detailed account, see Said 1980.
2. I wish to note that books that make the occasional reference to the Arab, but do not deal in any meaningful way with the "Arab problem" are not included in this selected shortlist.

1. Zionist Political Thought before Herzl

Political Zionism emerged well before the appearance of Herzl, but until the consolidation of his leadership, it had no significant influence on the Jewish masses.

The economic and political developments that took place in Europe from the latter half of the 18th century, specifically the French Revolution, the rise of nationalism, the Napoleonic wars, and the collapse of the feudal social order, directly affected Jewish life in Europe. Many of these developments related first and foremost to the question of the achievement by Jews of full civil rights as nationals of various European states. Napoleon's call in 1799 to Jewish communities in Asia and Africa, seeking their alliance in his Middle Eastern wars in return for support for the recovery of Jerusalem by the Jews and the recognition of the Jews as the chosen people with legitimate rights over Palestine, did not meet with any significant response (Kayyali 1970: 28-9; Laqueur 1972: 42; Cohen 121).

The advocacy by one of the leaders of the first Russian Revolution, Colonel Pastel, of a Jewish state in Asia Minor met similar failure (Laqueur 1972).

During this early period, against the background of the rise of capitalism in Europe and the correlative rise of the intellectual tradition of the Enlightenment, the first prominent Jewish voices were raised calling for the revival of Jewish nationalism and the establishment of a national homeland for the Jews. Their influence at that period was marginal. Among the prominent figures, one should mention Rabbi Yehudah Alkalai (1798-1878). Alkalai was influenced by the nationalist revival in Europe, and already in 1834 he began to publish articles on the subject of the redemption of the land of Israel, and a pamphlet, *Hear O Israel*. In this pamphlet, he proposed the establishment of Jewish colonies in the Holy Land. Most of his writings were addressed to wealthy Jews in the West, especially in France and England, aiming to mobilize their financial donations to purchase land in the Holy Land from the Turks, "As in biblical times Abraham had bought the field of Machpela from Ephron the Hittite" (quoted in Hertzberg 1976: 104).

Alkalai did not advocate simultaneous mass migration of all Jews to the Holy Land. In his pamphlet *The Offering of Yehuda*, Chapter 3, he writes:

We are therefore commanded not to attempt to go at once and all together to the Holy Land. In the first place, it is necessary for many Jews to remain for a time in the land of dispersion, so that they can help the first settlers in Palestine, who will undoubtedly come from among the poor. Secondly, the Lord desires that we be redeemed in dignity; we cannot therefore migrate in a mass, for we should then have to live like Bedouins, scattered in tents all over the fields of the Holy Land.

Redemption must come slowly. The land must, by degrees, be built up and prepared . . . . We are, alas, so scattered and divided today, because each Jewish community speaks a different language and has different customs. The divisions are an obstacle to the Redemption. (Hertzberg 1976: 105-7).

In the same pamphlet, Alkalai advocates the establishment of a world Jewish organization whose objective would be to promote the redemption of the land of Israel since without such an organization, redemption would not materialize:

The organization of an international Jewish lobby is in itself the first step to the Redemption, for out of this organization there will come a fully authorized assembly of elders and from the elders, the Messiah, son of Joseph, will appear. (Hertzberg 1976: 105-7)

Another important figure in this period was Rabbi Zeev Hirsch Kalisher (1795-1874). He came to develop a very similar advocacy to Rabbi Alkalai, although it is commonly believed that they had no contact throughout their lives. Kalisher lived in the district of Posen in the small township of Thorn in the northeast of Germany. He was a Reform rabbi, and like Rabbi Alkalai, he strongly advocated the establishment of Jewish colonies in the Holy Land with the support and sponsorship of their wealthy Jewish brethren. In 1836, Kalisher wrote a letter to the Rothschild family in which he said: "The beginning of the Redemption will come through natural causes by human effort and by the will of the governments to gather the scattered of Israel into the Holy Land" (Hertzberg 1976: 109-10).

In 1860 Kalisher joined a Jewish group in Frankfurt, Germany, organized by a certain Hayyim Lurie. The objective of this organization was to assist in the establishment of Jewish colonies in Palestine. Kalisher did not play an important role in this organization, but he did write a pamphlet in Hebrew published in Germany in 1862 under the title *The Seeking of Zion* (Kayyali 1970: 30; Hertzberg 1976: 110; Laqueur 1972: 52).

Kalisher held similar opinions to those advocated by Alkalai concerning the necessity of establishing a world Jewish organization to undertake the co-ordination of Jewish settlement in Palestine. He writes in *The Seeking of Zion*: "I would suggest that an organization be established to encourage settlement in the Holy Land, for the purpose of purchasing and cultivating farms and vineyards . . ." (Hertzberg 1976: 113)

Applying the inner logic of this line of thinking to the religious context, Kalisher concluded that the Messiah was indeed about to appear in the near future and it was therefore the obligation of the people of Israel to redeem the land of Israel and begin preparations for the reception of the Messiah. In his view the Messiah, when he comes, should find everything well prepared and ready for him. The Messiah should not be expected to gather the Jewish exiles from all parts of the world by last-minute improvisation; rather, the Jews must be ready.

> The Redemption of Israel, for which we long, is not to be imagined as a sudden miracle. The Almighty, blessed be His name, will not suddenly descend from on high and command His people to go forth. He will not send the Messiah from heaven in a twinkling of an eye, to sound the great trumpet for the scattered of Israel and gather them into Jerusalem. He will not surround the Holy City with a wall of fire or cause the Holy Temple to descend from the heavens . . . Israel would not return from exile at one time, but would be gathered by degrees . . . as the grain is slowly gathered from the beaten corn. (Hertzberg 1976: 113)

Unlike Alkalai who chose to disregard many aspects of the question, for example the Arab question although he had lived for a long period in Palestine, Kalisher attempted to address the issue and all of its relevant aspects. Despite the fact that he had never visited Palestine himself, he attempted to analyse how the other party, the Arabs, might respond. Whereas Alkalai's sole concern in this context was his fear that should Jews migrate to the country in large numbers, they might end up living like the bedouins (it will be interesting to see later how this image developed over the course of time), Kalisher was concerned with the problems that could develop through Arab opposition to Jewish settlement. Although he calls the native Arab population "robbers", he in no way disregards them: "Would not the property of the Jews in Palestine be insecure? Would not rapacious Arabs rob the Jewish peasants of their harvest?" (Laqueur 1972: 55).

This is the first time in the records of public political Zionist advocacy that the Arab problem is mentioned. Many leading thinkers and Jewish historians have claimed in their writings that they were not aware of the existence of the Arab people in Palestine. As we shall later see, one of the strongest claims of the Zionist movement was the claim that Palestine was vacant of population, and the powerful phrase was coined: "A people without a land for a land without a people". The phrase is attributed to the leading British Zionist, Israel Zangwill. The precise phrase seems to have been "the country was without a people waiting for a people without land" (Zangwill 1901: 627-31 quoted in Faris 1975: 81). This claim, however difficult to believe, is corroborated by the now classic article by the Jewish writer Ahad ha-Am, "Truth from the Land of Israel" (published 1891), in which he attacked Zionist propaganda on this point after his visit to Palestine. It is clear that Ahad ha-Am was not aware prior to his visit of the dimension of the problem, and that he became aware of the existence of the native Palestinian Arab population only when he had the opportunity to actually visit the country.

Whereas in this early period such awareness among thinkers and public figures may have been poor, clearly this was not the case in the period following the first Zionist Congress in Basel in 1897, as will be shown below.

It should also be noted that neither Alkalai nor Kalisher was interested in the establishment of a political Jewish state. Their main interest was the return to Zion and the preparation of the Jewish people for the coming of the Messiah. Undoubtedly, they have have realized that such a project could not be implemented except in the framework of a state, but this is not reflected in their writings. They did devote considerable effort to discussing details, especially how the Jews in Palestine could secure their livelihood and establish suitable conditions for the study of the Torah. Both reached the conclusion that it was necessary "to till the land with our own hands" (Kalisher), "to build houses, to sink wells, and to plant vines and olive trees" (Alkalai). Both also agreed that support of wealthy Jews must be mobilized and that this could only be done through the establishment of a world Jewish organization. This was indeed the course chosen later by Theodor Herzl.

Alkalai disregarded the Arab question of which he must surely have been aware, since he lived in Palestine for a certain period and called upon Jews to purchase the soil of the Holy Land from its non-Jewish owners. He did not, however, go into further detail.

The only concrete result of the efforts of these two rabbis, especially Rabbi Kalisher, was the establishment of a Jewish agricultural school near Jaffa called Mikveh Israel in 1870. This must be regarded as a spectacular achievement.

The third person of significance who involved himself in early Zionist advocacy was Moses Hess (1812-75). Hess was born in Berlin to Jewish parents and gained fame in his time largely through his socialist activities. In 1837, he published a book entitled *The Sacred History of Mankind,* which many historians consider to be the "first communist dissertation" (McLellan 1970: 14). Hess became a committed socialist after leaving Germany and his father's factory in the city of Cologne. McLellan comments on this book: "The book was mystical and meandering but contained quite clearly the idea of the polarization of classes and the imminence of a proletarian revolution" (1970:14).

Hess grew up as an assimilationist Jew, and he was not at all concerned with the Jewish problem until the latter period of his life (Taylor 1974: 9). He was a close friend of Marx and Engels, but this friendship began to deteriorate in the 1840s. Hess could not accept the kind of scientific socialism developed by Marx. Thus, in 1848, Hess was attacked in the *Communist Manifesto* where he is described by Marx disparagingly as a "true Socialist" (Samuel 1955:38).

This attack by Marx must have strongly affected Hess, and in 1852 he withdrew from politics and decided to devote himself to the study of the natural sciences (Laqueur 1972: 47). His opinions also changed. He was raised as an assimilationist Jew, and his first concern was for the proletarian class. In his first book, *The Sacred History of Mankind*, he wrote that the idea of a people chosen by God must disappear once and for all, and a better and more valuable life would then emerge. He took his ideas one step further when he wrote that if one has to opt for a religion, then one ought to opt for the Christian religion, which is more suited to modern times (Laqueur 1972: 48).

Hess returned to the Jewish arena and remained there for the rest of his life (McLellan 1970: 27). In 1862, the year Kalisher published his pamphlet *The Seeking of Zion,* Hess published independently and unexpectedly his book *Rome and Jerusalem: The Last Nationality Question.* In this book he apologizes for neglecting his people and distancing himself from their problems. The book begins with the following note:

> My way of return — after twenty years of estrangement, I have returned to my people. Once again I am sharing in its festivals of joy and days of sorrow, in its hopes and memories. I am taking part in the spiritual and intellectual struggles of our people and the gentile world. (Hertzberg 1976: 119)

Hess, who had devoted himself previously to the struggle against nationalism, now wrote:

> As long as the Jew denies his nationality, as long as he lacks the character to acknowledge that he belongs to that unfortunate, persecuted, and maligned people, his false position must become ever more intolerable. What purpose does this deception serve? The nations of Europe have always regarded the existence of the Jews in their midst as an anomaly. We shall always remain strangers among the nations. (Hertzberg 1976: 119)

This sentiment led him on more than one occasion to express disregard for or even insult other religions:

> To imagine that a recently manufactured prayer book or a hymnal which contains a philosophical theism put into rhyme and accompanied by music is more elevating and soul-stirring than the moving prayers in the Hebrew language which express the pain of our people at the loss of its fatherland . . . (Hertzberg 1976:124)

Hess soon reached the conclusion that it was necessary to establish a Jewish state. He considered the establishment of a state which would revive Jerusalem to be a historically necessary development of supreme importance: "The Jewish people will participate in the great, historical movement of present-day humanity only when it will have its own fatherland" (Hertzberg 1976:137)

Hess, who is reputed to have been a person of great moral sensitivity, did not see, as for instance Kalisher did, that there was another human and national question at stake since Palestine was already populated by another people. Despite all his anger at the European nations, he could not recognize that his own people were about to dispossess another.

Hess's book *Rome and Jerusalem* had no significance at the time of publication and probably no influence whatsoever. It sold 160 copies, and a year after publication Hess was obliged to purchase all the remaining stock from the publisher at reduced prices. Hess related the failure of his book to the economic situation of the Jews in Europe which was fairly good and in fact improved in that period: "The position of Jews in western society was certainly not critical; on the contrary it had immensely improved during those years. Within their communities, there were hardly any traces left of national spirit and enthusiasm" (Laqueur 1972:46).

In other words, the call voiced by Hess went against the economic interests of most Jews at the time. This may also explain why the book became popular only many years later with a deterioration of the economic position of Jewish communities and the crystallization of the national idea in Europe. It was against this background that the idea of a Jewish people that must be rehabilitated began to emerge, and then Hess's book became more important since it raised and debated the crucial subjects of the Jewish national question, the liberation of Jerusalem, and the role of Jewish religion in the fostering of Jewish national identity. Hess is considered to be the first prophet of Zionism; the first person to lay out the foundations of political Zionism (Cohen 42; Allen 1974:199-200; Taylor 1974:29; Al-Abid and Anza 1970:20)

As noted above, *Rome and Jerusalem* had a very limited circulation and no influence at the time of its publication. A similar fate had befallen a little pamphlet written by the Jewish doctor Leo Pinsker (1821-91), under the title *Auto-emancipation*. The ideas presented in this pamphlet were not new. But the analysis of the situation of the Jews in Europe, the call for Jewish self-help (since no one else would help them) and the call to establish a Jewish state — though not necessarily in Palestine — all contributed to make it much more significant than any other political Zionist document at the time of its publication (see Laqueur 1972:70-5; Taylor 1974:200; Al-Abid and Anza 1970:79).

Pinsker tried not to utilize the religious Jewish argument, unlike previous political Zionist writers. He saw the problem as a human problem. In principle he was sympathetic to the assimilation of Jews among the peoples in the midst of whom they lived. But in his opinion, this was impossible in practice:

> For the living, the Jew is a dead man; for the natives, an alien and a vagrant; for the property-holders, a beggar; for the poor, an exploiter and a millionaire; for the patriots, a man without a country; for all classes, a hated rival. (Hertzberg 1976:188)

He therefore advocated the establishment of a Jewish state as the only solution for the Jewish problem. Pinsker's call gained considerable attention among Jewish writers, especially in Russia, but did not have any influence whatever on the people at whom it was directed, especially German Jewry. When Pinsker discussed his views with the Chief Rabbi of Vienna, Rabbi Jellinck, the latter advised him to take a holiday in Italy to rest his strained nerves (Laqueur 1972:73).

In this period, the 1860s and after, until the advent of Theodor Herzl and the publication of his book *The Jewish State* in 1896, there emerged a number of thinkers and Jewish writers who further developed the political Zionist idea. Prominent among them are the writers Peretz Smolenskin (1812-85), Moses Lillienblum (1843-1910) and Eliezer Ben Yehuda (1858-1923). To the same period belongs A.D. Gordon (1886-1926) who developed the theory known as "the religion of labour". In his writings (see bibliography) he emphasized the importance of "the return" of Jews to Palestine, the establishment of Jewish settlements and the use of Jewish manual labour: these would transform the Jewish nation into a normal nation like all others throughout the world: "Only such a course will redeem the Jewish people," argued Gordon (Laqueur 1972:219). Gordon's influence proved to be seminal with the rise of labour Zionism as the dominant political force inside the Zionist movement, but generally speaking, the influence of early Zionist thinkers and advocates was limited. It is fair to say that political Zionism first emerged as a relevant and significant mobilizing force only under the leadership of Theodor Herzl and especially after the first Zionist Congress in the town of Basle, Switzerland, at the end of August 1897.

2. Political Zionism

The Zionist movement is a European political movement initiated in the latter half of the 19th century following the rise of the third estate, the European bourgeoisie, which replaced the feudal economic order in Europe with a capitalist regime (Leon 1972:246-7; Al-Azm 1970:86-7).

Correlatively, the feudal social and political order was replaced in Europe by the nation-state, rationalized by what has come to be termed "bourgeois nationalist ideology". It is against this context of economic, political and ideological development in Europe that the Zionist enterprise was formulated. As Abraham Leon points out: "In reality just so long as Judaism was incorporated in the feudal system the 'dream of Zion' was nothing but a dream and did not correspond to any real interest of Judaism" (Leon 1972:247). But with the radical dislocations in Europe and the destruction of the feudal order, the traditional place of Jewish communities in Europe was undermined. Zionism is one response to the crisis in which Jewish communities were subsequently situated: a secular response. The alternative secular response was Bundism. (See below.)

Zionism came to be predicated on three main assumptions: 1) the assumption of the spiritual tie of Jews to Palestine and the consequent use of Jewish religious attachment to Palestine in order to promote the political claim that the country belongs to the Jews on the basis of the biblical promise of the godhead to Abraham; 2) the identification of anti-Semitism as an inherent aspect of Gentile nature and the consequent claim that the only way of securing Jewish survival is the emigration of Jews from Gentile society to establish their own nation-state in Palestine; 3) the expression by the Zionist movement of the demand for national liberation to save all Jewish communities throughout the world from persecution and annihilation, and correlatively the claim that the Zionist movement is the sole legitimate representative of the Jewish people throughout the world.

There is no doubt that over the decades following the establishment of the Zionist movement at the first Zionist Congress in Basle in 1897, the movement was largely successful in achieving and consolidating these objectives as predicated on the three assumptions listed above.

In the framework of the Zionist enterprise and Zionist efforts to gain international support and recognition, three key themes were developed: 1) the presentation of Palestine as empty of population; 2) the warning that should the Jewish state not be established, the majority of Jews were likely to join socialist revolutionary movements; 3) the idea that a Jewish state would guard Western interests in the region against the Arab awakening, and in particular the routes to India which at the time were crucial for the European economy.

All three themes were successfully promoted in the West and until recently were incorporated into mainstream public opinion and national policy of most Western nation-states. It is therefore important to examine each of these three themes specifically.

A Country Empty of Population

The Zionist movement portrayed Palestine in the West as a country empty of population, except for a number of scattered bedouin tribes. This portrayal was firmly established and easily received since it was consistent with the standard racialist presentation of European colonial possessions. We therefore find in the literature expressions of surprise by leading Zionist figures and intellectuals when they came to realize that Palestine was populated: "But there are Arabs in Eretz Israel. I did not know this. We are therefore committing injustice" (Max Nordau, quoted in Elon 1971:151). Earlier, a similar observation had been made by the leading reviver of the Hebrew language, Eliezer Ben Yehuda, when he arrived in Palestine in 1882, and was "shocked to discover that the Land of Israel is now Arab" (Elon 1971:150).

Among these leading figures and intellectuals, some saw the truth and did not keep silent; rather, they warned that they were being misled. Prominent among them was Ascher Hirsch Ginsberg, a leading essayist, thinker and leader of the geopolitical Zionist Hibbat Zion movement, who used the pseudonym Ahad ha-Am. Following his visit to Palestine he published his essay "Truth from the Land of Israel" in 1891 in which he reported *inter alia* as follows:

> We abroad are used to believing that the Land of Israel is now almost totally desolate, a desert that is not sowed, and anyone who wishes to purchase these lands may come and purchase as much as his heart desires. But in truth this is not the case. Throughout the country it is difficult to find fields that are not sowed and sand fields and stone mountains that are not fit [to grow anything] but fruit trees, and this, also only after hard labour and great expense of clearing and reclamation — only these are not cultivated. (Ahad ha-Am 1965:23)

Yet the Zionist presentation of Palestine became, as noted above, the hegemonic conception popularized under the slogan attributed to Israel Zangwill, "The land without people for the people without land" (see p. 13, above).

The first Jewish Zionist immigrants to Palestine indeed reclaimed the land and drained swamps, since it was swamp and barren land that were cheapest to purchase and easiest to obtain. Yet despite massive Zionist mobilization of funds and efforts the total area purchased by Jews in individual or corporate capacities did not exceed 2% of Palestinian land in 1919 and 7% in 1946 (Khalidi 1971:841-3).

The Zionist presentation had to come to terms with a major inconsistency. It was difficult to argue that Palestine was empty of population and simultaneously come to terms with continuous native resistance, including military resistance. Still, as Edward Said pertinently points out and documents in *The Question of Palestine*, Zionist advocacy was consistent with Western epistemology on the Orient and the presentation could be sustained for many decades despite its inconsistency (Said 1980:15-55).

One of the main issues obsessing the architects of the Zionist efforts in Palestine and especially leading thinkers of the Zionist left was the demographic question: how to create a Jewish majority in Palestine? Thus the Zionist left, for instance, was fully aware of the fact that the creation of a class of farmers and workers as the mainstay for its conception of a "socialist" regime was a pre-condition of its success.

Many of the Jewish Zionist left leaders considered the implementation of Zionism to be the only route to the establishment of a "socialist" Jewish state. Thus Ber Borochov (1881-1917), who is often extolled as a "Zionist Marxist",[1] believed that:

> Zionism is a historical process. The future of the revolutionary class struggle of the Jewish worker is connected to the normalization of the conditions of national production and of his "strategic base" which will be achieved through the territorial concentration of the Jewish people in Israel; in other words, the Jewish working class can achieve socialism only through the fulfillment of Zionism. (Quoted in Cohen: 50-1)

The teachings of Borochov became the foundation for the Poelei Zion movement which at the time incorporated all Zionist tendencies which identified themselves as socialist. Still, this teaching, like all other Zionist teaching, had to confront an inherent problem. Aiming to achieve Zionist control over Palestine, it had to answer the question of the creation of a Jewish majority in Palestine.

Some of the Zionists thought they had found the logical solution to the problem by stipulating that the Palestinian Arabs and especially the Palestinian Arab peasants were mainly "Jews who were forced to convert their religion under the pressure of persecution and oppression" (Polk 1967:297). This view was prevalent among the second Zionist *aliya* (immigration) (1904-14), and its particular appeal was rooted in the "hope — the romantic, wishful thinking — that perhaps it would be possible in this fashion to maintain the Jewish majority in the country and that this majority only needs unification and fortification through propaganda and information" (Polk 1967:297).

In fact this was also the hope of Borochov, that the Arab majority would assimilate in the Jewish settlement with the expansion of the Jewish market and its modern technology.

A strong follower of this view was David Ben-Gurion, a founding leader of the state of Israel, head of the Jewish Agency, the Histadrut, and subsequently the first Prime Minister of the state of Israel. In 1917, Ben-Gurion published an article in one of the Jewish publications in New York under the title "Towards the Clarification of the Origin of the *Fallahin* [Palestinian Arab peasants]" in which he said:

> The Arab tribes who gained domination over Eretz Israel in the days of the Kalif Omar did not annihilate the agricultural population which inhabited the country at the time . . . The new rulers of the land did not themselves descend to till their estates: rather they left the former owners of the land to till the soil . . . The inhabitants of the villages which became subject to the new rule were the natives of the country that preceded the Arab conquest and who later adopted the language and the religion of the victors . . . Who were these farmers? The farming population which the Arabs found in Eretz Israel in the seventh century was none other than the Hebrew population which remained in its land . . . After the Arab conquest, the Arabic language became dominant and the religion of Islam gradually spread among the populace. The heavy burden of taxation which was imposed on the "infidels" under the "protection" of Islam, the Head Tax and the Land Tax from which the believers were exempt, motivated the non-Muslim inhabitants to accept the new religion. (Ben-Gurion 1917)

Israel Belkind is established as one of the heroes of the Zionist movement. He is also known to have devoted great interest to the demographic question of Palestine. He reached the same conclusion as David Ben-Gurion:

> Whereas we call the inhabitants of the country "Arabs", they do not refer to themselves by that name. If any one of them is asked: Who are you? he will answer: "Fallah", namely a tiller of the land, or a Muslim adherent to the Muhammadan religion. He will never identify himself as an Arab. By the name "Arab". . . he refers to the nomad Bedouin tribes which genuinely came from outside the country either as Arab conquerors or as those tribes known by the general reference of "the Sons of the East" who were the first to affiliate to the Arabs and adopt their new faith . . . The inhabitant of Eretz Israel knows and feels that though he speaks Arabic, the language of the foreign people who conquered the country 1300 years ago, he himself has not become an Arab . . . (Belkind 1969:17)

Thus Belkind concludes:

It is clear to us, therefore, that in Eretz Israel we encounter a good proportion of our people who, though they have ceased to share their lives with us for one thousand five hundred years, are still part of our flesh and bone. (Belkind 1969:23)

A.N. Polk was another scholar who occupied himself with the study of the origin of the Arabs of the country. He generally held a similar position to that of Ben-Gurion and Belkind, although his conclusions are more qualified:

Finally in the course of this process, a population was forged that can no longer be defined simply as Jews who became Muslim. This population has been well-integrated in the population of the neighbouring countries, yet there are strong ties of blood and origin between this population and the Jews, and the history of this population in Islam was marked by its memories of ancient Israel. (Polk 1967:303)

These views had strong opponents, of whom the most noted is the Israeli Jewish historian Abraham Jacob Brawer. Brawer strongly disagreed with Polk and argued that "the Arabs are an inferior and degenerate race; it is therefore inconceivable that this race has a Jewish element" (Brawer 1967-68:427)

The Threat of Jewish Participation in the Socialist Revolutionary Movement

Zionist enterprise and Zionist philosophy had developed in parallel with the rise and the articulation of Communist ideology in Europe and the organisation and formation of Communist parties. Given the specific social and political underpinning of Jewish existence in Europe, Communism strongly appealed to the Jewish audience, and Jews played leading roles in the advocacy and development of socialist thought. As Robert Wistrich notes:

Karl Marx was the creator of scientific socialism and the international Communist movement. Ferdinand Lassalle was the founder of the first German Workers' organization . . . Paul Singer was frequently chairman of the German Socialist Party Congresses. Edward Bernstein was the theorist of the reformist wing in German Socialism and the founder of "revisionism". Rosa Luxemburg was the leader of German and Polish left-wing Socialists and one of the founders of the German Communist Party . . . (Wistrich 1976:1-2)

The founder of political Zionism, Theodor Herzl, recognized the Jewish position on socialism in no ambiguous terms: "Educated Jews without means are now fast becoming socialists" (Herzl 1967:23). He did not hesitate to utilize the insight in his Zionist apologetics before the heads of state of imperial Europe and Turkey. Before the German Kaiser Franz Josef he noted: "The Zionist movement will do its utmost to distance the Jews from revolutionary parties which oppose the Kaiser" (Herzl 1960a: II, 173); and to the Ottoman Sultan, he proposed that a university be established in Turkey where Jewish lecturers would teach: "In order to distance the Turkish students from Western universities where they are brainwashed with revolutionary principles that are hostile to the interests of the Sultan" (Herzl 1960a: IV, 1275).

Similarly, one of the key architects of Zionist colonist settlement in Palestine, Arthur Ruppin, notes in his memoirs:

> As to Zionism I maintained a theoretical interest in the subject and already in 1897 and 1901 I visited a number of Zionist meetings; but I found them of no interest. . . . In these days in the years 1896-1899 I was under the influence of Karl Marx and his materialist conception of history. In every historical phenomenon I looked to see evidence to support the truth of this conception, and I was assisted by this conception in my study of Jewish history. . . . (Ruppin 1968:I, 201-4)

> Anyway, I very much respect the great idea that is at the foundation of Bolshevism, and I hope that this idea will not decline but quite the contrary will raise a contribution to world progress. Had I not been converted to Zionism I could see for myself no nobler object for my life than to offer my contribution to the formation of a new and peace-seeking regime in Russia. (Ruppin 1968:III, 29)

Jewish socialist organization was often outstandingly effective. The most important and most militant organization was the Bund which was very popular among the Jews in East Europe and was established as the first Jewish workers' party in Vilna in 1897 (the same year as the first Zionist Congress in Switzerland) as the General Union of Jewish Workers in Russia, Poland, and Lithuania. The Bund promoted among the mass of Jewish workers trade union militancy to improve their economic situation, as well as political activity and aggressive socialist propaganda (Talmi 1977:46).

Most Jews in East Europe belonged either to the working and artisan classes or to the liberal professions. Because of systematic discrimination against Jews at either end of the class polarity, socialist ideas and effective socialist organization gained ground among Jews in East Europe much faster than in Western Europe (see e.g. Mendelsohn 1970).

In the successive waves of Jewish emigration from East Europe following the pogroms of 1881, many leading members of the Bund settled in Western Europe. Consequently Herzl's call for the departure of Jews from Europe to Palestine to establish a Jewish homeland found responsive echoes among the leaders of the European regimes of his day.

Ezra Mendelsohn documents the following illustration:

> In Smozgon (a town in the Pale) for instance, a Jewish factory owner explained his policy of hiring Christians rather than Jews as follows: The Jews are good workers, but they are capable of organizing revolts . . . against the employer, the regime, and the Tsar himself.

Socialist and non-socialist observers alike argued that the Bialystok employers' fear of the Jewish workers' revolutionary potential led them to prefer the relative stability of the non-Jewish labour force . . . (1970:20)

The Defence of Western Interests in the Area

The Zionist movement knew that the West had important interests in the Arab region that sooner or later it was likely to lose. Hence the proposal that the envisioned Jewish state would act as a guardian for the West in the area.

We should remember that the Suez Canal (opened in 1869) was a crucial waterway for European trade and an important new short cut to India. The West was fully aware that the Ottoman Empire was declining and would soon collapse, and there were fears that it might be replaced by an Arab empire that would impose difficult conditions on the West. Herzl's advocacy and Zionist advocacy on this matter could not but be well received in the West (for details, see for instance Khalidi 1971: 125-42). The Zionist movement and the state of Israel have been consistent almost without exception in their support for Western powers in the international diplomatic arena as well. For instance, in 1952 when the Tunisian struggle for liberation was at its height Israel voted in the UN Political Committee with France and South Africa against Tunisia. It also voted against Algerian independence in 1953 and 1954.

It seems that the Western powers adopted Zionist logic on this crucial point and integrated Zionist positions into the framework of their own interests. Wishing to play it safe, however, the West, and especially Britain, made sure to establish ties with both parties. Thus Britain approached the Sharif Hussein, Emir of Mecca, and made it known in 1916 that the British Empire would be willing to provide assistance to the Arabs in their rebellion against Ottoman rule, and so help to secure Arab independence.

In this period the two Western superpowers, Britain and France, divided the Middle East into their respective spheres of influence under the Sykes-Picot agreement, concluded in 1916 and made public in 1919:

> Early in 1916, Sir Mark Sykes, who was attached to the Foreign Office as Advisor on Near Eastern Affairs signed an agreement on behalf of the British Government with François Georges Picot, representing the French Government, by which there was to be an Independent Arab state — or confederation of states — in the area known today as Saudi Arabia and Yemen Arab Republic: the French were to have control of Lebanon and Syria, the British that of Iraq and Transjordan. Palestine was to be under an international administration. This agreement was kept secret, because at the time of its signing it was thought that knowledge of it might prejudice the Allied cause. However, Tzarist Russia had been kept informed, and when the Bolsheviks came to power, they published the document, with consequent dismay and consernation among the Arabs. (Ingrams 1972: 2-3)

We now know that the British Colonial Office and the British government developed at the time a two-pronged diplomacy in the Middle East and two sets of incompatible commitments: on the one hand the commitment to the Arabs to support their independence (through Sir Henry McMahon's approach to Sharif Hussein), and on the other the Sykes-Picot agreement. Following these sets of commitments, the Balfour Declaration was issued on 2 November 1917 in the form of a letter from the British Minister for Foreign Affairs, Sir Arthur Balfour, to Lord Rothschild.

> Foreign Office
> November 2, 1917
>
> Dear Lord Rothschild,
> I have much pleasure in conveying to you on behalf of His Majesty's Government the following declaration of sympathy with the Jewish Zionist aspirations, which has been submitted to, and approved by the Cabinet.
> His Majesty's Government view with favour the establishment in Palestine of a national home for the Jewish people, and will use their best endeavours to facilitate the achievement of this object, it being clearly understood that nothing shall be done which may prejudice the civil and religious rights of existing non-Jewish communities in Palestine or the rights and political status enjoyed by Jews in any other country.
> I should be grateful if you would bring this declaration to the knowledge of the Zionist Federation.
>> Yours,
>> Arthur James Balfour
> (Quoted in Davis 1977:154)

The Balfour Declaration was a great victory for the Zionist movement. At the time very few raised the questions: by what right does England deliver a country that does not belong to the British people to a people that does not reside there? by what right does Britain deny the country to the resident native Palestinian population? Most revealing is the reference in the Declaration to the majority native population as "the non-Jewish communities in Palestine". A closer examination of the Declaration will reveal that Britain not only declared its intention to give the Palestinian Arab homeland to the Jews without seeking the consent of the native Palestinian Arab population, but, moreover, denied the native population any national rights, restricting their rights to the religious and civil spheres alone. When the contents of the Declaration became known in Palestine the response was bitter and translated itself into riots and revolts. When reports of these riots came back to London, it became clear that the Balfour Declaration might initiate a deep crisis between Britain and the Arabs and put British interests in the Middle East in danger (Kayyali 1970: 99-105). Some voices were raised in Britain itself against the Balfour Declaration, though admittedly these were few. Prominent among British opponents to the Balfour Declaration was the noted British historian Arnold Toynbee who wrote in 1918:

> Surely our foundation should be a Palestinian State with Palestinian citizenship for all inhabitants, whether Jewish or non-Jewish. This alone seems consistent with Mr. Balfour's letter. Hebrew might be made an official language, but the Jewish element should not be allowed to form a state within the state, enjoying greater privileges than the rest of the population. (Quoted in Ingrams 1972: 43).

We already noted that Zionism succeeded in this crucial period in distancing Jews from revolutionary commitment. When Herzl directed his efforts towards Western diplomacy, he was aware that Western states were not very happy about the waves of Jewish immigrants arriving from Eastern Europe, and especially from Russia and Poland after the mass pogrom against the Jews in 1881 which was instigated after the murder of Tsar Alexander II (1855-81) because a Jewish woman was among the conspirators (Kaufmann 1972: 190-4). Perhaps detailed attention should now be given to the work of the founder and first leader of political Zionism, Theodor Herzl.

Theodor Herzl

Dr Theodor Herzl (1860-1904) is considered to be the father of political Zionism. He was born in Budapest, Hungary, and completed his elementary education in a Jewish school there. He then went to a local secondary school until he was 15, whereupon he enrolled at the Anglican College and graduated in 1878. In the same year, his only sister died. His family decided to move to Vienna and Herzl enrolled at the University of Vienna and got his PhD in Law in 1884. (Jiryis 1977: 143; Zehavi 1967: 272-3).

Herzl began his career as a writer of short stories and plays. In 1885 one of his plays was shown in New York City. Later, in 1891, he joined the editorial board of the Austrian *Neue Freie Presse,* considered at the time to be the best Austrian daily. The owners of the paper were two liberal Jews. In the course of his work for the paper, he was sent to Paris where he was posted for four years as correspondent. In 1895 he returned to Vienna and became the paper's literary editor, a post he held for the rest of his life (Jiryis 1977; Bein 1961:30-49).

Herzl's personal background was not Zionist nor was hs family religious in the orthodox sense of the term. His father had no contact of consequence with the Lovers of Zion movement. His grandfather was an observing Jew, but Herzl himself was alienated from the Jewish tradition, like most Jewish youth at this time (see Jiryis 1977: 44). Herzl very much identified with and was proud of his Germanic background. In one of the sessions of the third Zionist Congress in a heated discussion on Jewish education, Herzl asked disparagingly: "What is Jewish education?" (Herzl 1960a: V, 12-13).

Herzl read Pinsker's *Auto-emancipation* only after the publication of his book *The Jewish State,* and he read Hess's *Rome and Jerusalem* only during his visit to Palestine in 1898 (Herzl 1960a: III, 1090). The most important influence on Herzl's thinking was the book by the anti-semite Duhring Eugen (Herzl 1960a: III, 1090). The other related influence on his thinking was the Dreyfus affair in France. Dreyfus was a French army officer of Jewish background. He was charged with high treason, and during the public hearing, Paris was ridden with demonstrators carrying banners: "Death to the Jews! Death to the traitors!" Among the prominent figures to mobilize in the defence of Dreyfus was the noted French writer, Émile Zola. Herzl finally concluded that it is of no consequence how the Jew defines his own person. Most important is how the majority of the population defines the Jew, even if the Jew himself has completely cast off Jewish identity or religion (Friedman 1977:11).

This became Herzl's fundamental point of departure on the basis of which he began to organize his activities. He focused on the question of finding a patron for the Jewish problem. His first step was to seek wealthy Jews who would back the idea of the Jewish state. Towards this end, he met Baron Hirsch, a wealthy French Jew, to whom he expounded his plan to establish a Jewish state through the purchase of an area somewhere in the world where Jews could reside. But Baron Hirsch rejected the notion and called the meeting to a close, without even giving Herzl the courtesy of hearing his presentation to the end (Herzl 1960a: 7,9-10; see also Jiryis 1977: 146).

Herzl departed in great disappointment and very depressed, but he resolved to organize his thoughts and present them in writing as well as organizing a group of supporters: the result was the pamphlet, *The Jewish State*. The book was published on 14 February 1896, when Herzl was 36 years old. When he received the first parcel of his books, he entered in his *Diaries:* "My 500 copies came this evening. When I had the bundle carted to my room, I was terribly shaken. This package of pamphlets constitutes the decision in tangible form. My life may now take a new turn" (quoted in Laqueur 1972: 84).

The Jewish State
The point of departure of the Jewish state is the ingathering of the Jews into a single territory:

> The Jewish question still exists. It would be foolish to deny. The Jewish question exists wherever Jews live in perceptible numbers. Where it does not exist, it is carried by Jews in the course of their migration. We naturally move to those places where we are not persecuted and there our presence produces persecution. This is the case in every country and will remain so even in those highly civilized, for instance, France — till the Jewish question finds a solution on a political basis. (Herzl 1967: 14-15)

Herzl declared that:

I think the Jewish question is no more a social than a religious one, notwithstanding that it sometimes takes these and other forms. It is a national question which can only be solved by making it a political world question to be discussed and settled by the civilized nations of the world in council. (Herzl 1967)

Where will this state be established? "Let the sovereignty be granted to us over a portion of the globe large enough to satisfy the rightful requirements of a nation; the rest, we shall manage for ourselves" (Herzl 1967: 28).

Herzl portrays the local native population of the area, namely the Arabs, as if they were barbaric in the crudest sense of the term. As we shall see later, this portrait of the native Palestinian Arab has become a fundamental point of reference for the Zionist movement. In order to implement his vision, Herzl concluded that the only realistic option was to adopt the established patterns of European imperialism and colonialism of his day; he therefore proposes in his pamphlet to establish two Jewish companies, the Society of Jews and the Jewish Company.

The Society of Jews will do the preparatory in the domains of science and politics which the Jewish Company will afterwards practically apply. The Jewish Company will see to the realization of the business interests of departing Jews and will organize commerce and trade in the new country. (Herzl 1967)

Herzl proposed two preferred territories, Argentina and Palestine, but he adds: "We shall take what is given to us" (1967: 30). Herzl, however, eventually realized that Palestine would attract many more Jewish immigrants than any other prospective territory because:

Palestine is our ever-memorable historic home. The very name would attract our people with a force of marvellous potency . . . Supposing his Majesty, the Sultan, were to give us Palestine, we could in return undertake to regulate the whole finance of Turkey . . . We should there [in Palestine] form a portion of the rampart of Europe against Asia, an outpost of civilisation as opposed to barbarism. We should as a neutral state remain in contact with all Europe which would have to guarantee our existence. (Herzl 1967)

In *The Jewish State* Herzl drew a blueprint of the state which he aspired to establish. He wrote on the laws, the regime, the armed forces and security, labour, the conquest of the land, language, and he even drew the flag of the state: "I would suggest a white flag with seven golden stars". (Herzl 1967: 72). He went a little bit too far when he wrote: "But the Jews, once settled in their own state, would probably have no more enemies" (Herzl 1967). Did Herzl really believe that an empty territory could be found anywhere in the world or that the native population of the territory designated for the Jewish state would fail to resist such encroachments?

Herzl was not the first to advocate and promote the idea of establishing a

Jewish state. We have discussed above the contribution of some of his noted predecessors, namely, Alkalai, Kalisher, Hess and Pinsker. Herzl recognized and acknowledged this fact. The Russian Jewish writer Ahad ha-Am wrote that Herzl's *The Jewish State* gave him the feeling that he was reading the ideas expounded by Pinsker translated from the language of the ancient prophets to the language of modern journalism (Ahad ha-Am 1965: 171).

Herzl attempted to organize a group of people around his ideas but during the eight years that remained to him after the publication of *The Jewish State* he laboured very much alone. He did, however, succeed in gathering around himself a number of Jewish student organizations in Vienna. Two people who assisted him crucially were Max Nordau (1840-1923) and David Wolfson (1856-1914). The first was born in Budapest and was eleven years Herzl's senior. At their first meeting, Herzl felt that they were stealing ideas from each other (Jiryis 1977: 146).

Nordau was a physician by profession and a noted author in his day. It was very important for Herzl to have Nordau on his side. David Wolfson was a timber merchant from the city of Cologne and one of the leaders of the German Lovers of Zion movement. He had solid roots in Judaism and considerable status in German Jewish society (see Laqueur 1972: 100).

These were Herzl's first two important supporters. They aided him in the organization of the first Zionist Congress which convened in Basle, Switzerland, on 29-31 August 1897.

The resolutions taken at this Congress guided the development of the Zionist movement throughout its history. Those resolutions were as follows:

> Zionism seeks to establish for the Jewish people a home in Palestine, secured under public law. The Congress contemplates the following means to the attainment of this end:
> 1. The promotion by appropriate means of the settlement in Palestine of Jewish farmers, artisans and manufacturers.
> 2. The organization and uniting of the whole of Jewry by means of appropriate institutions, both local and international, in accordance with the laws of each country.
> 3. The strengthening and fostering of Jewish national settlement and national consciousness.
> 4. Preparatory steps towards obtaining the consent of governments, where necessary, in order to reach the goal of Zionism. (Israel Pocket Library 1973: 82; see also Laqueur 1972: 106; Jiryis 1977: 155).

These resolutions were taken as if Palestine was void of population. There is no mention of the native people resident in the country. Whereas in the very early period of political Zionist history, such disregard could be attributed to genuine ignorance, since the facts of the situation and the concrete conditions in Palestine may have been largely unknown, now, after the first Zionist Congress and reports such as that by Ahad ha-Am, "Truth from the Land of Israel", such disregard was consciously assumed and cultivated. It was only when the Palestinian Arabs began to organize forceful opposition to the conquest of their lands that the Zionist movement was compelled to depart from its position of consciously cultivated and artificial disregard of the native Palestinian Arab population and begin to confront in explicit terms what came to be designated as "the Arab problem".

At the time, Palestine was under Ottoman rule and so Herzl thought it appropriate to begin negotiations with the Ottoman authorities. In order to obtain audience with Sultan Abd Al-Hamid II, he contacted two people who were reputed to have good connections with him: Nuri Bey, the director of the Ottoman Foreign Office, and Arminius Vambery, who was one of the Sultan's courtiers. Herzl met Sultan Abd Al-Hamid II on 17 May 1901; and offered to provide Jewish financial assistance to extricate Turkey from its dire economic state (Friedman 1977: 96-100).

In February 1902, Herzl was asked to travel to Istanbul where the administration informed him that it was willing to permit free Jewish immigration to all parts of the Ottoman Empire on condition that the immigrants accept Ottoman nationality. "They would be permitted to establish themselves in any part of the Ottoman empire except Palestine" (Friedman 1977: 96-100; Jiryis 1977: 161).

The proposal could hardly appeal to Herzl, being inconsistent with the Zionist aspiration of settlement in Palestine and the establishment of a Jewish national home there. Then Herzl failed to mobilize funds to support his commitment to the Ottoman Sultan. When the Zionist leadership realized that nothing much could be expected to come out of the negotiations with the Ottoman administration and that the Ottoman Empire was fast disintegrating, it altered the focus of its efforts, redirecting them towards England. To underline this new orientation, the fourth Zionist Congress (1900) was held in London and attracted much attention in the British administration.

Herzl continued with his efforts in the fields of international relations. He was received for audience before Victor Emmanuel III, the Italian monarch, who told him: "Palestine will and must get into your hands . . . It is only a question of time" (Friedman 1977: 111). In 1898 Herzl met the German Kaiser and presented his plans. But the Kaiser's response was negative, and he notified Herzl that he would be unable to assist him with his efforts in the Ottoman court (Jiryis 1977: 164). In the same period, Herzl was also received for audience with Pope Pius X, who also rejected Herzl's notions and programme, and refused to recognize the Jews as a people.

Herzl died on 3 July 1904. He did not see the establishment of the Jewish state in Palestine or elsewhere in the world, but he prophesied that such a state would indeed be established within 50 years of his death. His prophecy came true.

Israel's ties with the West did not terminate after the establishment of the state of Israel; on the contrary, the ties were consolidated, and it became increasingly clear that Israel was acting against the interests of the Arab East as an ally of the West. One example is the 1956 war when Israel allied itself with France and England to combat Arab nationalism as represented by the Egyptian President, Gamal Abdul Nasser, who had just nationalized the Suez Canal controlled by the West for the previous century.

One ought to note that prior to the establishment of Israel, liberal and, to a more limited extent, radical and socialist circles were swayed by the argument that Jewish ties with the West could be manipulated to bring about the establishment of the state, which would subsequently become truly independent. Those who advocated or supported this argument genuinely failed to understand that such an abstract analytic separation between Zionism and imperialism was only supported by shaky empirical evidence. That the issues were clearly understood is illustrated by the now classic editorial written by Gershom Schocken, the editor and owner of Israel's Hebrew liberal daily *Ha'aretz*, in 1951:

> The second motive for the West to support us financially is in that the West is not very happy with its relations with the other states in the Middle East. The feudal regimes in these states are forced to take in considerable consideration movements (secular and religious) which often have a clear leftist social colour, to the extent that such states are no longer willing to make their natural resources available to Britain and the United States, nor allow them the use of their countries as military bases in the case of war. Indeed, the ruling circles in Middle Eastern countries are fully aware that in the event of a socialist revolution or Soviet occupation, they are doomed to physical annihilation. But the immediate fear of the bullet of a political assassin overshadows for the time being the less concrete fear of annexation to the communist world. All these states are weak militarily. Israel has demonstrated its military strength in the war of Independence against the Arab States and therefore a certain strengthening of Israel is a fairly convenient way for the Western superpowers to maintain a balance of the political forces in the Middle East. By this opinion, Israel is designated the role of a kind of watchdog. There is no fear that it will initiate aggressive policies against the Arab States should such initiative stand in clear contradiction to the desire of the United States and Britain, but should the Western powers choose for one reason or another to turn a blind eye one can trust that Israel will be able to properly punish one or any number of its neighbouring states whose lack of propriety against the West would have exceeded the permissible bounds. (Schocken, *Ha'aretz*, 30 September 1951; Quoted alos in Bober 1972: 16-17).

Note

1. I cannot accept this description since in my view "Zionist Marxist" is a contradiction in terms.

3. The Establishment of the State of Israel in 1948

When Hitler became the Chancellor of Germany on 30 January 1933, the smell of war was in the air. The world feared it:

> The man who rose all of a sudden to power in Berlin was the very same man who for many years ridiculed the accepted international order, elevated violence to the level of method in the political struggle and dragged all the ethical values of the western world in the mud. (Ben Elissar 1978:17)

The new international climate had direct implications for the conflict in Palestine. Britain was determined to put the conflict to an end at all costs in order to concentrate all its political attention on the new developments in Europe.

In 1939 World War II began and brought the situation in Palestine under a new focus. Hitler's concentration camps made Jewish migration to Palestine "legitimate" in many eyes throughout the world. Palestinian Arab opposition did not find anybody of significance in the West who was willing to lend an ear to their case.

The Zionist movement lost no time. It had no wish to lose any of the sympathy gained as a result of World War II. It attempted to capitalize maximally on the favourable conditions for the establishment of a Jewish state.

> Immediately after the end of the war, on 27.5.45., the executive of the Jewish Agency petitioned the British government to declare Palestine a Jewish state. It also submitted a programme for a free and democratic Jewish Commonwealth to the San Francisco Conference of the United Nations. (Laqueur 1972: 564)

Britain refused to commit itself to such a statement since it already had incompatible commitments to its Arab allies. Towards 1947, the British position in the Palestine conflict became increasingly untenable and Ernest Bevin, British Foreign Secretary, took the issue for resolution by the United Nations General Assembly (Ben-Gurion 1971: 63).

In an unexpected development, the Soviet Ambassador to the UN declared as follows:

> It would be unjust to ignore the desire of the Jews for an independent state of their own, or to deny them the right to realize that goal. This would be unjustifiable particularly in view of what the Jews suffered during the Second World War. (Ben-Gurion 1971:63)

This position was apparently based upon an assessment that a Jewish state under the hegemony of one or a number of left-Zionist parties would offer the Soviet Union the opportunity to establish a foothold in the Middle East, at a time when all other Middle East countries were ruled by anti-Communist regimes which did not allow any Communist organization. This assessment proved wrong and resulted in one of the worst mistakes in Soviet foreign policy.

The UN General Assembly established a Special Committee to investigate the situation in Palestine. The committee visited Palestine in June 1947, and published its report in September of the same year. Among its recommendations were the following:

> 1. The Mandate for Palestine shall terminate, as soon as possible but in any case not later than 1 August, 1948.
> 2. The armed forces of the Mandatory Power shall be progressively withdrawn from Palestine, the withdrawal to be completed as soon as possible but in any case not later than 1 August, 1948.
>   The Mandatory Power shall use its best endeavour to ensure that an area situated in the territory of the Jewish state, including a seaport and hinterland adequate to provide facilities for a substantial immigration, shall be evacuated at the earliest possible date and in any event not later than 1 February, 1948.
> 3. Independent Arab and Jewish States and the Special International Regime for the City of Jerusalem set forth in Part III of this plan, shall come into existence in Palestine two months after the evacuation of the armed forces of the Mandatory Power has been completed, but in any case not later than 1 October, 1948. The boundaries of the Arab state, the Jewish state, and the City of Jerusalem shall be as described in Parts II and III below.
> 4. The period between the adoption by the General Assembly of its recommendation on the question of Palestine and the establishment of the independence of the Arab and the Jewish states shall be a transitional period. (Tomeh 1978:4-5)

On 29 November 1947, the UN General Assembly endorsed the recommendations of the Special Committee with the necessary two-thirds majority. The Arab states who cast their votes against the resolution also announced their intention to frustrate its implementation, threatening to use force of arms in order to prevent the establishment of a Jewish state in the land of Palestine. On the date of the adoption of the resolution the Arab Higher Committee announced a three-day general strike. Fighting erupted almost immediately. In his speech before the Zionist General Council on 4 April 1948, David Ben-Gurion stated: "Over 900 Jews have been killed in the four months since the Arab attacks began on November 30 [1947], the day after the U.N. General Assembly decided on the establishment of a Jewish state in part of the country" (Ben-Gurion 1971:67).

Britain announced that it would terminate its mandate on Palestine on 15 May 1948. On 14 May 1948, at 4.30 p.m., the Jewish National Committee convened in Tel Aviv to make the "Declaration of Independence", under which the independent state of Israel was established.

> The State of Israel will be open to the immigration of Jews from all countries of their dispersion; will promote the development of the country for the benefit of all its inhabitants; will be based on the principles of liberty, justice, and peace as conceived by the prophets of Israel; will uphold the full social and political equality of all its citizens, without discrimination of religion, race, or sex; will guarantee freedom of religion, conscience, education and culture; will safeguard the Holy places of all religions, and will loyally uphold the principles of the United Nations Charter. (Laqueur 1976:159-62)

Following the departure of the British administration and army from Palestine on 15 May 1948, the 1948 war broke out. Three days earlier the Political Committee of the Arab League had met and recommended that its member states declare war on the Jews in Palestine. Thus on 5 May 1948, the armies of Egypt, Jordan, Syria, Iraq and Lebanon moved into Palestine (see Allush 1970:160-1; Robnett 1968:215-17; Ben-Gurion 1971:102-3).

The Arab armies lost the war. The Israeli armed forces were better equipped and by far superior in organization; also, the Jewish community could mobilize more soldiers on the battlefield than the five Arab states together.

The newly established state of Israel was officially committed to the UN 1947 Partition Plan for Palestine. However, by deliberate design, under the cover and the pretext of the claim (correct in itself) that all Arab states rejected the said UN resolution, the new state embarked upon a project of occupation and expansion into territories well beyond those allocated to the Jewish state in the 1947 Partition Plan.

Well before the departure of the British mandate authorities from Palestine, the unofficial Israeli armed forces, the Haganah, the Irgun, and the Lehi, all embarked upon the conquest of localities and territories beyond the boundaries of the Jewish state as defined by the UN Partition Plan. The following register was compiled on the basis of news reports, as published in the *New York Times:*

Name of locality	Conquest
Qazaz	21 December 47
Sasa	16 February 48
Salama	1 March 48
Bir Adas	6 March 48
Kana	13 March 48

Al-Kastal	4 April 48
Deir Yasin	10 April 48
Lajjun	15 April 48
Saris	17 April 48
Tiberias	20 April 48
Haifa	22 April 48
West Jerusalem	25 April 48
Jaffa	26 April 48
Acre	27 April 48
Safad	7 May 48
Beit Shean	9 May 49

(Quoted in Al-Abid 1970: 91).

During the war, some strata of Palestinian Arab society, predominantly the rich and sections of the middle classes, left the country to establish residence in the neighbouring countries, but the overwhelming majority of the population was forcibly expelled by the armed forces of the Jewish community in Palestine which, following the declaration of the establishment of the state of Israel on 15 May 1948, were officially constituted as the Israeli army (Israeli Defence Forces). In addition to forcible expulsion, the Palestinian Arab inhabitants were subjected to a systematic campaign of terrorization. One of the more widely known examples of this campaign was the massacre in the village of Deir Yasin by the Irgun and the Lehi of over 200 men, women and children on 9 April 1948. The survivors were taken captive and marched in a "victory parade" through the streets of Jewish West Jerusalem (Cohen 395 fn).

The story of the expulsion and the dispossession of the Palestinian Arab people from their homeland is now adequately researched and published (e.g. Waines 1977; Abu Lughod 1971; Sayigh 1979; Davis, Mack and Yuval-Davis 1975). It is instructive, however, to quote in this context a Zionist eyewitness account. Musa Goldenberg, senior official for the Jewish National Fund, who followed closely the course of events in his own district, the Beit Shean district, entered in his memoirs the following:

> The [Arab] inhabitants of Beit Shean turned angrily to their leaders with the demand that they hasten the surrender before the city is completely destroyed. Some of the notables who were seated next to me consulted with me as to how they should reply and what was my opinion. I told them only that if they surrendered and avoid war, they could pursue their occupations without disturbance and save helpless people and gain the blessings of thousands of women and children. The decision was taken to surrender without fighting. The police station was immediately evacuated from its police units and I saw to it that they did not take out the weapons which were concentrated in the building. Emissaries were sent out from the city and met with the delegates of Moshe Mann [presumably the military commander of the area] . . .
> One day the order came from the central command to evacuate the city of

Beit Shean immediately of its Arab residents because the regional defence centre was to be based there. I know that the reason given for the evacuation would not be correct, but I had no course of appeal, and I could not even properly reflect upon the matter. The fighting was still raging, and an order is an order. I drove to Beit Shean since I had to explain to its inhabitants — 700 people — the importance of this arrangement, and I thought I could sweeten the bitter medicine by offering some concessions and promises that would make it easier for the inhabitants to follow the order. The day came and announcements were made throughout the streets of Beit Shean that every inhabitant could choose either to travel to Nazareth by buses provided by the Israeli government or emigrate to Trans-Jordan with the commitment that our army would guarantee their safety until the bridge of Sheikh Hussein. Either way the city had to be completely evacuated by the following evening.

The city was struck with severe panic. Strong abuse was voiced against the state of the Jews which persecutes the inhabitants unnecessarily. I tried to explain that this was merely a provisional order and that matters will settle down soon but no one listened to me. In order to lend force to the evacuation order a Piper airplane flew over the city and threw bombs on the courtyards where concentrations of inhabitants could be seen, inflicting death and injury. Afterwards, soldiers marched through the town in something like a demonstration of strength and hurried the people to depart. Only a small proportion, perhaps one quarter of the inhabitants, chose to go to Nazareth. The remainder of the population chose to go into exile . . .

When I returned to Beit Shean, I found the city completely empty of Arabs. Many people [namely Jews] from far and near descended on the homes and looted valuables, most commonly carpets, furniture, radio sets, etc. . . . And thus the majority of the inhabitants from Beit Shean walked in long convoys packed with their belongings, their backs bent, old men as well as children on the road to the Sheikh Hussein Bridge, heading towards Trans-Jordan. A number of young soldiers of the Israeli army escorted the exiles and some of them prodded them rudely, hitting them with the butts of their guns. I rebuked them furiously, but they did not heed my rebukes and pushed them more and more rudely. Overnight, we became masters over lands and water . . .
(Goldenberg 1965:202-5, 219)

The case of Beit Shean was not unique. Numerous similar cases are recorded throughout the country, for instance the expulsion of the inhabitants of Lydda and Ramleh in June 1949 (El-Asmar 1978; Jones 1975; *New York Times,* 23 October 1979), the expulsion of the inhabitants of Haifa (Mu'ammar 1958), and the massacre of Duwayma. This last case being relatively unknown deserves full reference:

I wish to submit to you an eyewitness report given to me by a soldier who was in Duwayma on the day following its occupation . . . He opened his heart before me because there are not many hearts these days that are willing to listen. He arrived in Duwayma immediately after its occupation. The conquering army was Battalion 89 . . . They killed some 80-100 Arabs: women and children. The children were killed smashing their skulls with clubs. There was not a single house without dead. The second wave of the army consisted of the

Battalion of the soldier who gave this eyewitness report . . . In the village there remained Arab men and women who were put in the houses without food or drink. Then the sappers came to blow up the houses. One officer ordered a sapper to put two old women into the house he was about to blow up. The sapper refused and said that he will obey only such orders as are handed down to him by his direct commander. So the officer ordered his own soldiers to put the old women in, and the atrocity was carried out. Another soldier boasted that he raped an Arab woman, and then shot her. Another Arab woman with a day old baby was employed in cleaning jobs in the yard . . . She worked for one or two days in the service, and then she was shot together with her baby . . . Cultured and well mannered commanders who are considered good fellows . . . turned into low murderers, and this happened not in the storm of the battle and blind passion, but because of a system of expulsion and annihilation. The less Arabs remain — the better. (Kafkafi 1979)

Al-Duwayama was a large Muslim village, 17 km west of Hebron with 2,700 residents. It was destroyed in 1948. In 1955 Kibbutz Amatziyah was established on the site by a nucleus of Israeli-born and Anglo-Saxon new immigrants. The settlement has since altered its status to a small-holders' co-operative or *moshav*.

Detailed records of the expulsion of Palestine Arab communities throughout the territories that were later to come under Israeli sovereignty are now published (Jiryis 1976; Davis and Mezvinsky 1975). During the 1948 war and its immediate aftermath, 385 Palestinian Arab villages and towns inside what was to become pre-1967 Israel were destroyed by the Israeli army. The inhabitants of these villages and towns constitute the majority of the Palestinian Arab refugee population. The lands owned and cultivated by this population before the 1948 war were handed over to *moshavim* and kibbutzim for exclusive Jewish cultivation, rationalized and made legal through appropriate legislation passed in the Israeli Parliament (for details see Jiryis 1976).

The expulsion and exile of the Palestinian Arab people from their homeland was deliberate and formalized in the notorious Plan D, issued as the official strategic framework for the Israeli army in the 1948 war.

Ironically, the fate of those Palestinian Arabs who remained under Israeli rule, in so far as their property rights are concerned, was no better than the fate of the hundreds of thousands of Palestinian Arab refugees who were doomed to exile for over three decades. Musa Goldenberg's eyewitness report is again illuminating:

In the city of Nazareth an unbearable situation was created. Thousands of Arabs who fled through fear of the war from their homes assembled in Nazareth and waited for the storm to pass. Meanwhile, their villages were deserted and also the authorities began razing them with bulldozers. There were villages which were saved this fate in recognition of the contribution of their inhabitants who collaborated with our military authorities, and were therefore spared. They were the happiest people in the country. But the destiny of those who fled to the city or crossed temporarily to Trans-Jordan with their relatives, or fled to neighbouring villages and after some time returned to their native village to regain occupancy of their lands and their homes was to be different. A clerk on behalf of the military government registered all present inhabitants on the day of census in the village and those present were given temporary certificates for Israeli citizenship. The rest, who appeared and claimed emphatically that they were absent for only one or two days from the village were rejected, and their claims disregarded. Thus a large body of Arabs was formed which was registered as absentees in the registry of the military regime, and their property confiscated. Sometime later they were registered as Israeli residents, but their property was not returned to them, and they were dubbed with the strange name of "present absentees". This was the case of the residents of Beit Shean, who evacuated the city "temporarily" at the request of the army as well as other villages and towns. (Goldenberg 1965:208-9)

Goldenberg's eyewitness report is misleading in one sense: in most cases, even collaborating villages were not spared. The well-known case of the two collaborating villages of Bir'im and Iqrit is the best documented example to date. Both of the villages were razed to the ground and their inhabitants became refugees inside the state of Israel (present absentees). (For details, see Davis and Mezvinsky 1975).

The Israelis desperately attempted to rationalize the enormity of the injustice perpetrated against the native Palestinian Arab population by claiming that the local Palestinian Arab inhabitants left Palestine of their own volition and that one could not possibly blame the Jews for the fact of the Arab departure.

As I noted above, specific narrow sectors of the Palestinian Arab society — the richer sectors — indeed left the country, with the intention of returning after the fighting subsided. In either case, however, the Zionist claim must be challenged on grounds of principle: is it justifiable to claim that the fact that a person leaves his or her place of residence in time of war or, for that matter, in time of peace constitutes a necessary and sufficient condition for that person to lose his or her rights to property and residence?

Official Zionist and Israeli agencies claim that the Arab leadership urged the inhabitants to leave in order to return later, behind the victorious Arab armies who would successfully expel the Jews. This claim is untrue. The British writer and journalist Erskine Childers published a study on the subject in 1961 in which he pointed out, *inter alia*:

Israel claims that the Arabs left because they were ordered to, and deliberately incited into panic by their own leaders who wanted the field cleared for the 1948 war . . . The Arabs charge that their people were evicted at bayonet-point and by panic deliberately incited by the Zionists.

Examining every official Israeli statement about the Arab exodus, I was struck by the fact that no primary evidence of evacuation orders was ever produced. The charge Israel claims was "documented", but where were the documents? There had allegedly been Arab radio broadcasts ordering the evacuation, but no dates, no names of stations, or texts of messages were ever cited. In Israel in 1958 as a guest of the Foreign Office and thereby doubly hopeful of serious assistance, I asked to be shown the proofs. I was assured they existed, and was promised them. None had been offered when I left, but I was again assured. I asked to have the material sent on to me. I am still waiting . . .

As none of the other stock quotations in Israeli propaganda are worth comment, I next decided to test the undocumented charge that the Arab evacuation orders were broadcast by Arab radio — which could be done thoroughly because the BBC monitored all Middle East broadcasts throughout 1948. The records and companion ones by a U.S. monitoring unit can be seen at the British Museum.

There was not a single order or appeal, or suggestion about evacuation from Palestine from any Arab radio station inside or outside Palestine in 1948. There is a repeated monitored record of Arab appeals, even flat orders, to the citizens of Palestine — to stay put. (Childers 1961:672-5)

The Palestinian Arab people were expelled and exiled from their homeland. Almost overnight the overwhelming majority of the Palestinian Arab people in the territories that came under Israeli rule became refugees. The continued existence of Israel as a Jewish and a Zionist state determines for the Palestinian Arab people the loss of their homeland: the Palestinians were made refugees and exiles whereas the Jews established for themselves an exclusively Jewish state.

Prior to the establishment of the state of Israel, the leaders of the Zionist movement boasted at all international forums that they were committed to establishing a democratic state which would guarantee equality of rights to all its inhabitants without distinction of religion or nationality. (See the text of the Israeli Declaration of Independence above.)

The leaders of the Zionist movement repeatedly claimed that the Arab inhabitants of the country would become equal citizens of the Jewish state. Thus for instance, before the Anglo-American Committee of Inquiry on Palestine, on 26 March 1946, David Ben-Gurion testified that the Jewish state would have two functions:

> One: the function to care for the welfare of the people of this country, all of them without any difference between Jews, Arabs or others, to care for their security, to work for their welfare and to raise them higher and higher economically, socially and intellectually. The other function is to continue building a National Home.
> We will have to treat our Arabs and other non-Jewish neighbours on the basis of absolute equality as if they were Jews, but make every effort that they should preserve their Arab characteristics, their language, their Arab culture, their Arab religion, their Arab way of life, while making every effort to make all the citizens of the country equal civilly, socially, economically, politically, intellectually and gradually raise the standard of life of everyone, Jews and others. (Quoted in Lustick 1980:37-8)

In a memorandum to the United Nations Special Committee on Palestine in

1947, the Jewish Agency repeated these assurances:

> What will be the character of this State? It will be an independent self-governing Palestinian State with a Jewish majority, in which all citizens, regardless of race or creed will enjoy equal rights, and all communities will control their internal affairs. The State will not be Jewish in the sense that its Jewish citizens will have more rights than their non-Jewish fellows, or that the Jewish community will be superior in status to other communities, or that other religions will have an inferior rank to the Jewish religion . . . A Jewish majority in Palestine necessarily implies that non-Jews will form a minority of the population; it does not imply that they will be reduced to what is commonly known as "minority status". (Lustick 1980)

Moshe Sharett (Shertok), the general director of the Political Department of the Jewish Agency, in his testimony before the Anglo-American Committee of Inquiry, on 26 March 1946, said:

> Palestine as a Jewish State implies no superior status for the Jews save in one respect: the right of entry [e.g. the Law of Return]. Inside the State there will be complete equality of rights for all inhabitants regardless of race or creed, complete eligibility of all for all offices, up to the highest . . . I repeat, no privileges, no superiority of status, no special rights for the Jews of Palestine or for the Jewish religion or for any Jewish institution. (Quoted in: Davis, Mack and Yuval-Davis 1975: 198-9; Lustick 1980:37)

The general import of the statements proclaimed by the official spokespeople of the Zionist movement prior to 1948, as illustrated above, clearly committed the movement to a Jewish state which would guarantee equality of rights to all its inhabitants with one single exception, namely the right of Jewish "return". It is illuminating to subject these statements to factual examination.

Official British mandate statistics for 1947 determine the Arab population of Palestine at 1,319,434, versus 589,341 Jews (Abu Lughod 1971: 155). After the establishment of the state of Israel in 1948 (and before the conclusion of the armistice agreements in 1949), only 117,639 Palestinian Arabs remained in the territories which came under the control of the state of Israel. One year later, in 1949, the Palestinian Arab population under Israeli rule increased to 160,000 as a result of the annexation of the Palestinian villages of the Triangle handed over to Israel in the framework of the 1949 armistice agreements with Jordan (Abu Lughod 1971: 155).

In 1949 the Palestinian Arab community under Israeli rule constituted 13.6% of the total population of the state of Israel. The bulk of this population was concentrated in three districts: approximately 60% in Galilee, approximately 30% in the Triangle, and just under 10% was the bedouin population in the Negev; the remainder of the Arab communities were in the major cities of Haifa, Acre, Lydda, Ramleh, Jaffa and Jerusalem (Jiryis 1976: 5).

The Palestinian Arab community in Palestine following the 1948 war and the establishment of the state of Israel was transformed overnight from being members of a majority people in their homeland to being a national minority dispossessed of their land and properties and severed from the mainstream of their people. Most families were ripped apart. Some stayed under Israeli occupation but the majority of the population was expelled across the border and became refugees in Jordan, Lebanon, Syria and the Gaza Strip. Those who remained under Israeli occupation were subject not only to severe material injustice and measures of radical political repression, but also to the constant humiliation imposed on them by an arrogant Jewish David who had successfully defeated an Arab Goliath in the 1948 war. The overwhelming majority of the Jewish citizens of the state of Israel were euphorically committed to Zionism and cared little for the fate of the Palestinian Arab people, let alone that of those Palestinian Arabs who remained under direct Zionist occupation.

When it appeared that a certain section of the Palestinian Arab people had remained in their homeland and were unlikely to leave; when it appeared in parallel that under the prevailing international circumstances it was not possible to engineer the mass expulsion of this population, or an exchange with their neighbouring Arab states in return for Jewish communities resident in neighbouring Arab countries, then the newly established Israeli authorities chose to deal with the "Arab problem" in their midst by subjecting the Arab population to a military regime (Jiryis 1976: 4).

The legal framework for the military regime was set by the Defence (Emergency) Regulations, 1945, originally introduced by the British mandate authority and subsequently incorporated by the Israeli Parliament (Knesset) into the body of Israeli law. These regulations empowered the military governors to apply any measure they deemed necessary at their complete discretion. Through these regulations the military governors were legally empowered to harass, restrict and consistently repress every form of social and political activity inside the Palestinian Arab community and effect massive confiscation of the lands of those Palestinian Arab villages which remained under Israeli rule (Qahwaji 1972; Jiryis 1976; Landau 1971; El-Asmar 1978; Zureik 1979; Lustick 1980).

The body of the legislation known as the Defence (Emergency) Regulations, 1945, consolidates earlier legislation, specifically the emergency regulations first introduced by the British mandate authority in 1936 in its attempt to crush the Great Arab Rebellion (1936-39). These regulations were consolidated in 1945 and applied by the British mandate authorities against the various Zionist underground organizations in an attempt to counter the united rebellion launched earlier in that year.

The Jewish community in Palestine strongly opposed these regulations. On 7 February 1946, some 400 Jewish lawyers convened in Tel Aviv to demonstrate their protest and opposition. Dr Moshe Dunkelblum, later to become an Israeli Supreme Court judge, made the following statement:

It is true that these laws threaten every Jewish settler, but, as lawyers, we are especially concerned because they violate the basic principles of law, justice, and jurisprudence. They give the military and administrative authorities absolute power which, even if it had been approved by a legislative body, would create a state of chaos . . . The Defense Regulations abolish the rights of the individual and grant unlimited power to the administration. The aim of this conference is to express our position, both as settlers, and as lawyers, on these laws which rob every settler of his basic rights, in violation of law, order and justice. (Quoted in Jiryis 1976:11)

And similarly, Dr Bernard Joseph, later to become Minister of Justice, announced his condemnation in no less vigorous terms:

As for these defense regulations, the question is: Are we all to become victims of officially licensed terrorism or will the freedom of the individual prevail? Is the administration to be allowed to interfere in the lives of the people with no protection for the individual? As it is, there is no guarantee to prevent a citizen from being imprisoned for life without trial. There is no protection for the freedom of the individual, there is no appeal against the decision of the military commander, no means of resorting to the Supreme Court . . . while the administration has unrestricted freedom to banish any citizen at any moment. What is more, a man does not actually have to commit an offense; it is enough for a decision to be made in some office for his fate to be sealed . . . The principle of collective responsibility has become a mockery. All of the six hundred thousand Jewish settlers could be hanged for a crime committed by one person in this country.

A citizen should not have to rely on the goodwill of an official, our lives and our property should not be placed in the hands of such an official.

There is no choice between freedom and anarchy. In a country where the administration itself inspires anger, resentment, and contempt for the laws, one cannot expect respect for the law. It is too much to ask of a citizen to respect a law that outlaws him. (Quoted in Jiryis 1976:11-12)

Another participant, Advocate Jacob Shimshon Shapira, who subsequently succeeded Dr Bernard Joseph as Minister of Justice, was even more emphatic:

The established order in Palestine since the defense regulations is unparalleled in any civilised country. Even in Nazi Germany there were no such laws and the [Nazi] deeds of Maidanek and other similar things were against the code of laws. Only in an occupied country do you find a system resembling ours. They try to reassure us by saying that these laws apply only to offenders and not to the whole of the population, but the Nazi governor of occupied Oslo also said that no harm would come to those who minded their own business . . .

It is our duty to tell the whole world that the Defense Regulations passed by the government in Palestine destroy the very foundations of justice in this land. It is mere euphemism to call the military courts "courts". To use the Nazi title, they are no better than "Military Judicial Committees Advising the

Generals". No government has the right to draw up such laws . . . (Quoted in Jiryis 1976)

The body of the Defence (Emergency) Regulations, 1945, consists of some 170 separate articles which together subject every detail of Palestinian Arab social and political life in Israel to the arbitrary administrative discretion of the military governor.

The best summary of this draconian legislation is available in the English translation of Sabri Jiryis's classic dissertation, *The Arabs in Israel*. One can hardly hope to improve on his work, and thus it is in order to quote him on this subject extensively:

> The defense regulations themselves, worded in great detail, are a typical example of the traditional imperialist attitude in dealing with the native population of a colony. They give the authorities extensive and extremely rigorous powers and their enforcement can destroy individual freedom and individual rights to property almost completely. They cover every aspect of life, from control over the freedom of speech, movement, and the press to the regulation of the possession of arms, the expropriation of property, and the control of means of transportation. Some of their more important provisions are as follows.
>
> Concerning freedom of expression, Article 142 states that "any person who endeavours whether orally or otherwise, to influence public opinion in a manner likely to be prejudicial to public safety, defense or the maintenance of public order" shall be considered as having committed a crime. Similarly, Article 109 (I)(d) says that restrictions can be imposed on any person "in respect to his employment or business, in respect of his association or communications with other persons, and in respect of his activities in relation to the dissemination of news or the propagation of opinions". In addition, "no notice, illustration, placard, advertisement, proclamation, pamphlet or other like document containing matter of political significance . . . shall be printed or published in Israel" without first obtaining a permit. The district commissioner can grant or refuse the permit "without assigning any reason therefore" (Articles 94 and 96). The press censor has the right to prevent the publication of any material he considers harmful to the security of the nation or the welfare of the people. He can forbid the importation or distribution of such material and force editors, printers, writers, and journalists to submit all articles for his approval before publication. Articles 122 and 126 empowered the military governor to "prevent, limit, or supervise . . . the use of specific roads or roads generally"; Article 129 enabled him to "order the owners or foremen of stores and workshops . . . should he have reason to believe that they have been shut as a result of a general or organized strike . . . to reopen them and work as usual . . . or conversely . . . order the shops shut for a determined period"; Article 119 allowed him to "order the confiscation . . . of any house, building, or piece of land if he has reason to suspect that guns have been fired . . . or bombs, explosives, or fire illegally set off from that property; and the confiscation of any house, building, or piece of land lying within a region, town, village, neighbourhood, or street if he is convinced that the inhabitants of that region, town, village, neighbourhood, or street have

committed, attempted, or aided and abetted a crime or were accessories after the fact to a crime."

The Israeli authorities did not, in fact, use the above-mentioned powers against the Arabs except in rare cases and in emergencies. For reasons to be explored later, they preferred other articles. The most notorious was Article 125 which "grants the military governor the power to proclaim any area or place a forbidden [closed] area . . . which no one can enter or leave without . . . a written permit from the military commander or his deputy . . . failing which he is considered to have committed a crime". Thus all the Arab villages and settlements in Galilee, the Triangle, and the Negev were divided into small pockets called "closed areas", usually consisting of one or more Arab villages, which no Arab could leave or enter for any reason without first obtaining a written permit from the military governor of the area. (Jiryis 1976:16-18)

With the establishment of the Zionist movement, a clear goal was formulated which has not altered to this day, namely to obtain lands in Palestine at any price and by any means for exclusive Jewish settlement. Thus, Menachem Ussishkin (1863-1941), a leading Zionist, founder member of the Lovers of Zion movement, chairman of the Board of Directors of the Jewish National Fund and the recognized father of Jewish agricultural settlement in Palestine, wrote as follows:

In order to found autonomous Jewish community life, or more precisely a Jewish State in the Land of Israel, at least most of the Land of Israel must be the property of the people of Israel. Without ownership rights of the land, the Land of Israel will never become Jewish whatever the number of Jews in the country, in the cities, and even in the villages may be. Without ownership rights to the land, the Jews will be placed in the same abnormal position as in the lands of their dispersion . . . We must embark immediately on the project of purchasing land in the Land of Israel. It is necessary that the redemption of the country be made our slogan at this time: to purchase, obtain and reclaim in every way and by all means available to us land of any type whatsoever. (Shmueli 1961)

In 1948, after the establishment of the state of Israel, the Israeli government took possession of all state domains including lands held by Arab villages in common ownership (Musha'a) and registered in the name of the British mandate High Commissioner on behalf of the villages concerned.

In order to legalize the seizure of lands registered by the Ottoman and the British mandate Lands Registry (Tabu) under the individual title of their owners (both those owners who were made refugees outside the state of Israel and those who remained under Israeli rule) the Israeli Parliament passed in March 1950 the "Absentees' Property Law", which stipulates as follows:

1. In this Law:—
(a) "Property" includes immovable and movable property, monies, a vested or contingent right in property, goodwill and any right in a body of persons or

in its management.

(b) "Absentee" means:—

(1) A person who, at any time during the period between the 16th Kislev 5708 (29 November, 1947) and the day on which a declaration is published, under section 9(d) of the Law and Administration Ordinance, 5708-1948 that the state of emergency declared by the Provisional Council of State on the 10th Iyar, 5708 (19 May 1948) has ceased to exist, was a legal owner of any property situated in the area of Israel or enjoyed or held it, whether by himself or through another, and who, at any time during the said period:—

(i) was a national or citizen of the Lebanon, Egypt, Syria, Saudi-Arabia, Trans-Jordan, Iraq or the Yemen, or

(ii) was in one of these countries or in any part of Palestine outside the area of Israel, or

(iii) was a Palestinian citizen and left his ordinary place of residence in Palestine

(a) for a place outside Palestine before the 27th Av, 5708 (1 September, 1948): or

(b) for a place in Palestine held at the time by forces which sought to prevent the establishment of the State of Israel or which fought against it after its establishment;

(2) A body of persons which, at any time during the period specified in paragraph (1), was a legal owner of any property situated in the area of Israel or enjoyed or held such property whether by itself or through another, and all the members, partners, shareholders, directors or managers of which are absentees within the meaning of paragraph (1), or the management of the business of which is otherwise decisively controlled by such absentees, or all the capital of which is in the hands of such absentees. (*Laws of the State of Israel*, p.98 (Hebrew) 1950)

The implications of this law are draconian in the extreme. The law institutes a Custodian of Absentees' Property and vests all property defined under this law as "Absentees' Property" under his complete authority. It is virtually impossible to challenge successfully the ruling of the Custodian and it is sufficient that the Custodian issue a certificate in writing to the effect that a person or a body of persons is an "Absentee" under the stipulation of the law in order that that person or body of persons shall, so long as the contrary has not been proven, be regarded as an "Absentee".

In other words, a Palestinian Arab citizen of the state of Israel who is physically present in the state of Israel can be declared under the said law an "Absentee" on the grounds, for instance, that during the period specified in the law he had at any time left his ordinary place of residence (e.g. left Jaffa for Nazareth). The law makes it incumbent upon the person declared an "Absentee" by the Custodian to prove the contrary, which under the terms of this legislation is almost impossible. Individual persons and corporate bodies declared "Absentees" under this law, even if present in the state of Israel, thereby lose all rights to their urban and rural properties. According to the *Israeli Government Year Book, 1958*, the properties vested in the Custodian included 350 evacuated or partly evacuated Arab villages in a total area of

3,125,000 dunams (Cohen n.d. 325).

In parallel the Defence (Emergency) Regulations, 1945, were similarly applied with the object of seizing lands under Arab ownership and cultivation. Instrumental in this regard is Article 125 which stipulates as follows:

> A military Commander may by order declare any area or place to be a closed area for the purposes of these Regulations. Any person, who, during any period in which any such order is in force in relation to any area or place, enters or leaves that area or place without a permit in writing issued by or on behalf of the Military Commander shall be guilty of an offence against these Regulations.

(For detailed accounts, see El-Asmar 1978: 16-17; Jiryis 1976: 89-90.)

The legislation developed by the Parliament of the state of Israel in order to facilitate the seizure of Arab lands and transfer these lands to exclusive Jewish cultivation and ownership is by now long and quite impressive. It is outside the scope of this study to undertake a legal exposition of this subject but detailed studies have been made (see Jiryis 1976; Davis, Mack and Yuval-Davis 1975; Cohen; Lustick 1980; Zureik 1979).

It is important to note that the Arabs strongly resisted the expropriation of their lands. The resistance was expressed inside the state of Israel by large demonstrations, sit-ins, persistent cultivation of the confiscated land despite the issuing of writs of confiscation, and appeals through the courts by Arab citizens against the government (Israel Yearbook 1966-67: 201). Outside the borders of the state of Israel the resistance is now well institutionalized in the body of the PLO.

The repression of the Palestinian Arab population who remained under Israeli rule has its origins in the Zionist idea itself. In order to establish and maintain a "Jewish state", it was necessary to draw legal distinctions between Jew and non-Jew, and to guarantee privileges to the Jewish citizens of the state. These aims could only be achieved at the expense of the non-Jewish, namely Palestinian Arab, citizens and at the cost of subjecting them to systematic discrimination, legal as well as political. In the following I intend to concentrate on the question of political freedom which is one of the central foundations of any regime that claims to be democratic. The violation of the norms of political freedom, the application of policies of political repression, are profoundly significant in the case of the Palestinian Arab citizens of the state of Israel in that, in the social and political climate created by policies of systematic political repression, many of the individuals concerned were motivated to consider emigration or illegal activity. I submit, and I hope in the following to support the argument, that these have been explicit motives in Zionist thinking on the matter.

Since the establishment of the state of Israel, and throughout the period of this study (1948-75), there have been seven separate attempts by Arabs to found separate Arab political parties to participate in Israeli parliamentary elections. These initiatives were led by Arabs of various ideological and political affiliations. Yet common to all seven initiatives is the fact that they were effectively aborted by the Israeli authorities well before they had the opportunity to test their viability in election campaigns. The seven attempts were led by: 1) Daud Khuri (Nazareth), 1951; 2) Muhammad Nimr al-Huwari (Nazareth), 1951; 3) Niqula Saba (Haifa), 1951-52; 4) Muhammad Nimr al-Huwari (Nazareth), Abdallah Khayr (Daliyat al-Karmil), and Elias Qusa (Haifa), 1955; 5) Masa'ad Qasis (Mi'iliya), 1959; 6) Abu Laban (Jaffa), 1960; and 7) Al-Ard, 1964.

In all cases the authorities applied strong pressures on the members of these groups to compel them and their supporters to withdraw. It was clear that the authorities would not allow an independent Arab party to be formed inside the state of Israel. In the case of Al-Ard, when the pressures proved inadequate, the authorities declared the organization illegal, and the Israeli Supreme Court of Justice obligingly issued a verdict to that effect (Jiryis 1976: 185-202; Landau 1971: 91-3; Zureik 1979: 172-5).

In parallel, the authorities have consistently supported the formation of Arab parties affiliated to Zionist parties which guaranteed complete subservience and fostered moral and material corruption inside the Arab sector.

Amnon Lynn, then the head of the Department for Arab Affairs in the Labour Party, explained the position of his party, on the question of the establishment of an independent Arab party inside the state of Israel as follows:

> The mere existence of an Arab party that is not dependent on the Jewish parties constitutes a danger because experience in the Middle East indicates that inside nationalist parties the most extreme elements invariably prevail; the moderate and sober elements are removed and denounced as "traitors" . . . a nationalist party that does not identify with the State could eventually wreak disaster on the Arab population in Israel. (*Ha'aretz*, 5 January 1967)

The Zionist parties represented in Parliament knew well how to manipulate "their Arabs". The control of their Arab affiliates was so detailed as to determine the nature of their speeches before the House.

> It could be argued that the list of Arab candidates affiliated to Mapai [Labour] resemble private groups rather than political parties. Their main task is to obtain Arab support for Mapai in the elections on the one hand, and vote in support of the Party at crucial divisions in the Knesset on the other. And indeed the Arab members of Knesset affiliated to the Jewish Mapai Party have carefully avoided as a general rule dealing in their speeches with subjects such as the military regime or Israeli relations with the Arab States.
>
> The co-ordination committee for minorities in the Knesset consisted of five Jewish members of Knesset of Mapai, and its task was to meet whenever necessary with the Arab members of Knesset affiliated to the Party to listen to

their demands, maintain negotiations and co-ordinate their speeches and their voting in line with that of the other Party members of Knesset. (Landau 1971: 95-6)

In my own view, the considerations outlined by Landau are the main reasons why all Israeli governments refuse to allow independent Arab party organizations inside the state. Other non-party independent organizations are subject to similar procedures: all Israeli universities refuse to recognize the Arab Students' Committees and the Union of Arab Students' Committees in Israel, whereas all cultural and ethnic Jewish societies in these universities obtain immediate recognition and support. Arab students in Israeli universities are barred from numerous university departments and are not eligible for scholarships stipulating as a requirement completion of compulsory military service. (For detailed discussion of the situation of Arab students in Israeli universities, see Amun *et al.* 1977, Zureik 1979; Nakhleh 1979).

The emergence of the Palestine Liberation Organization (PLO) and the achievement by the PLO of international recognition as the sole legitimate representative of the Palestinian Arab people, culminating in the invitation to the PLO Chairman Yasser Arafat to address the UN General Assembly on 13 November 1974, profoundly affected all sections of the Palestinian Arab people including that section now totalling over 600,000 people under Israeli rule since 1948. A new political focus emerged inside Israel based on the recognition of the PLO as the sole legitimate representative of the entire Palestinian Arab people including those who happened to be citizens of the state of Israel (El-Asmar 1978). The response of the authorities to these developments was predicated on intensified repression: thus, the proposed Congress of the Arab Masses, called by the Israeli Communist Party, Rakah, in Nazareth on 6 December 1980, was banned by Prime Minister Menachem Begin according to his powers under the Defence (Emergency) Regulations, 1945 (*Haolam Hazeh*, 10 December 1980). Similarly, the Israeli authorities have placed the leadership of the Abna Al-Balad (Sons of the Country) movement and the National Progressive Movement under house arrest since June of the same year (*The Committee for the Defense of Political Prisoners in Israeli Jails* (mimeo), Umm al-Fahm, Israel, September 1981).

In conclusion it seems that all governments of the state of Israel have demonstrated extreme insecurity in the face of independent Palestinian Arab political and ideological challenge, and have thus invariably opted for policies of legal and administrative repression against the Palestinian Arab population which remained under Israeli Jewish rule. It seems further that if such measures are necessary in order to defend the Zionist argument in the political debate inside the state of Israel, then its moral, social and political foundations must be very shaky indeed.

4. The Non-Existent Palestinian Arab

Clearly the Zionist movement was compelled sooner or later to confront the Arab question. In the context of having to come to terms with the Palestinian Arab reality in the "Promised Land", the existence of the Palestinian Arab had to be eliminated or radically reduced. Without such reduction, the Zionist argument could not possibly assume its tenuous credibility. Needless to say, such credibility was predicated on a completely false and grossly distorted perception of the Arab in all relevant domains: cultural, political, psychological.

As we have noted above, in the early stages of the Zionist movement, namely from the middle of the 19th century until the turn of the 20th century, the Palestinian Arabs were hardly mentioned in Zionist literature. Rabbi Kalisher was the first Zionist to mention the Arab, albeit only in a single paragraph expressing his concern for the safety of the property of Jewish immigrants in Palestine in view of possible Arab attacks (Laqueur 1972: 55). With the exception of this mention, there is complete disregard in Zionist literature of the fact that Palestine was populated and that its native population was Arab until the publication of Ahad ha-Am's crucial article "Truth from the Land of Israel" (Ahad ha-Am 1965).

Historians are divided on this question. Some argue that most leading Jewish intellectuals and Zionist advocates were genuinely not aware of the Palestinian Arab reality in the Holy Land. They point to Ahad ha-Am's article, as well as to comment by Nordau and Eliezer Ben-Yehuda as corroborative evidence.

It is clear, however, that in many important ways, Ahad ha-Am's article marks a watershed, and that whereas Zionist disregard for the Palestinian Arab question prior to its publication could have been genuine, subsequent avoidance of the question was consciously and politically motivated.

Thus we know that Herzl's deliberate avoidance of the mention of the "Arab problem" was not based on ignorance. Already in 1899 Herzl corresponded with Yusif Al-Din Al-Khalidi, who was then a member of the Ottoman Parliament and the head of the Jerusalem Municipal Council. This correspondence was initiated by Al-Khalidi who addressed a letter to the

Chief Rabbi of Paris, Rabbi Zadok Cohen, where he says that he considers it his moral duty to warn Zionists about Arab hostility to the conquest of Palestine and proposes that the Zionist movement address itself to a different territory (Elon 1971: 162).

Rabbi Zadok Cohen forwarded the letter to Herzl who then wrote back to Al-Khalidi. Still, both in his *The Jewish State* and in his memoirs, Herzl completely ignored the Palestinian Arab. There are only two references in Herzl's writing to the Arabs; one in his diaries, referring to the suggestion by Eliezer Ben-Yehuda of publishing a Zionist newspaper in Arabic. Herzl thought that the idea was not bad at all (Herzl 1960a: II, 804). The second is in Herzl's novel *Altneuland,* where a reference is made to Rashid, an Arab who lives peacefully and amicably in the future Zionist state (Herzl 1960b: 126-35; see also Jiryis 1977: 191).

A number of prominent Zionist leaders did leave written records of the moral dilemma placed before their conscience by the existence of the Palestinian Arab people in the land designated by the Zionist movement for Jewish redemption. Thus Arthur Ruppin, who, in the period from 1908 to 1931 in his capacity as the director of the Palestine office of the Jewish Agency, was the supreme architect of Zionist colonization and settlement in Palestine, soon came to realize that his Zionist commitments and his general humanistic commitments were incompatible:

> It became clear how difficult it is to realize Zionism and still bring it continually into line with the demands of general ethics . . . On every site where we purchase land and where we settle people, the present cultivators will inevitably be dispossessed . . . The Arabs do not agree to our venture. If we want to continue our work in Eretz Israel against their desires, there is no alternative but that lives should be lost. It is our destiny to be in a state of continual warfare with the Arabs. This situation may well be undesirable, but such is the reality. (Ruppin quoted in Davis 1977: 55-6)

Ruppin was aware of the inconsistency quite early in his career. Already in 1923 he entered in his diary: "I feel that I cannot continue to work in the Zionist movement if Zionism is not given a new theoretical foundation. Herzl's concept of the Jewish state was possible only because of his disregard for the Arab presence" (Ruppin 1968: III, 77).

Arthur Ruppin is exceptional among the Zionist leadership in that he achieved quite a realistic assessment of the force and significance of the Arab nationalist aspiration. He began to accuse his colleagues in the Zionist leadership of total disregard for the Arab problem which he identified as being the central problem for the Zionist movement. In his diaries he entered on 21 January 1921:

> I sometimes find myself now in doubt whether Zionism has altogether survival capacity . . . The fact that the Arabs of Eretz Israel are hostile to Zionism despite the consistent policy of reconciliation pursued by Herbert Samuel [British High Commissioner to Palestine] depresses me greatly. I believe that

without better understanding with the Arabs, we will first face enormous obstacles that can almost be impossible to overcome. (Ruppin 1968: III, 14)

How did Ruppin think of solving this problem? We find in his diaries an entry dated 30 May 1928: "The situation would have been different had there already been among the Arabs a party, be it a small party, which would be reconciled in principle with the Zionist activity." (Ruppin 1968: III, 153).

Joseph Weitz, long-time chairman of the JNF (Jewish National Fund) and Arthur Ruppin's successor as architect of Zionist colonization from the 1940s to the 1970s, was less perceptive. In his diaries he notes:

> What did these people [Palestinian Arabs] do here? All they did was to expand the swamps, to increase disease, to raise thorns and thistles over thousands of dunums of fertile land, to be nomads with their herds and, despite their hard labour, live a life of poverty, pressure, and misery. Is it not the case that they ought to make place to a flourishing culture which can support ten people where now one lives? (Weitz 1965: I, 41)

Ruppin, like all other members of the Zionist executive, knew full well that the Arabs would not be willing to reconcile themselves to Zionist activity which has always aimed and still aims to expel and dispossess the Palestinian Arabs and turn them into refugees in order to make way for the Zionist movement to establish, support and expand the Jewish state.

Although Ruppin, and a few other Zionist leaders, recognized in the Arabs a major factor in the conflict with whom a settlement must be achieved since they "also" have rights in Palestine, most Zionist leaders refused to acknowledge Arab rights in Palestine and consistently denied that any people other than the Jewish people has any rights in Palestine.

In one of their meetings, the noted scientist Albert Einstein asked Haim Weizmann, the first President of the state of Israel: "What about the Arabs if Palestine were given to the Jews?" Weizmann answered "What Arabs? They are hardly of any consequence" (quoted in Booth 1969).

Levi Eshkol, the former Prime Minister of Israel (1963-69) said in an interview with *Newsweek*: "What are Palestinians? When I came here, there were 250,000 non-Jews, mainly Arabs and Bedouins" (*Newsweek,* February 1969). In reality Eshkol migrated to Palestine in 1913, when the Arab population totalled some 600,000 (Bowle 1957: 77).

Also in 1969 Golda Meir made a similar statement:

> There was no such thing as Palestinians. It was not as though there was a Palestinian people in Palestine, considering itself as a Palestinian people, and we came and threw them out and took their country away from them. *They did not exist.* (*Sunday Times,* 15 June 1969; emphasis added)

Thus in one single breath, Mrs Golda Meir disposed of the existence of an entire people.

It is in order to note that in Zionist terms of reference and official political language, the Egyptian Arabs are Egyptian, the Iraqi Arabs are Iraqi, the

Syrian Arabs are Syrian, the Jordanian Arabs are Jordanian, etc., but the Palestinian Arabs are Arab. They are not recognized, and in so far as the Zionists are concerned, they do not exist.

Let us immediately note that the issue of whether Herzl or any other Zionist leader mentioned or failed to mention the Arab presence in Palestine has no ultimate significance. The important issue is the complete and consistent disregard for Palestinian Arab rights in the constitution and practice of the Zionist movement and the Zionist agencies. The Zionists predicated all their plans on the assumption that Palestine was free of population and that the Arabs did not exist. All funds and all institutions within the framework of a Zionist movement were reserved exclusively for Jews by constitution and by practice. An important and typical illustration is the constitution and practice of the central organizational body of socialist labour Zionism, namely the Histadrut, popularly known abroad since 1948 as the Israeli General Federation of Labour.

The Histadrut was established in December 1920 as the General Federation of the Hebrew Workers in the Land of Israel, and it was defined as: "the national organization of Hebrew workers in Eretz Israel to promote their professional economic settlement and cultural interests in order to establish the society of Hebrew labour" (Talmi 1977: 99).

Clearly by title and by programme, the Histadrut officially and explicitly excluded Arab workers' participation. This so-called socialist vanguard of the Jewish working class in Palestine was predicated on the institutional exclusion of Arab workers from its concern, thus clearly abrogating any form of socialist commitment to class solidarity and brotherhood among nations. The official programme of the Histadrut as established in 1920 consistently echoes a basic programmatic commitment of all the labour Zionist parties, including the most radical labour Zionist party at the turn of the century, Hapoel Ha-Tzair (The Young Worker), whose 1905 platform read as follows:

> 1. To defend the interests of the Hebrew workers in Eretz Israel, to increase their numbers and to improve their economic situation.
> 2. The conquest of labour by the Jewish worker, the organization of work and the investigation of labour conditions.
> 3. Assistance to the activity of Zionist settlement through the provision of knowledge and important facts.
> 4. Concern to adjust the institutions in the country and their activities so that they correspond to the aspiration of the people.
> 5. Concern to improve the economic and the cultural situation of the Jews of Eretz Israel.
> 6. Concern to make the Hebrew language in Eretz Israel the ruling language. (Merhav 1967:37)

The name of the Histadrut remained unaltered after the establishment of the state of Israel in 1948 and the incorporation of a significant minority of Palestinian Arabs as citizens of the newly established Jewish state.The Histadrut's official title remained the General Federation of the Hebrew

Workers in the Land of Israel until as late as 1966. It was only then, and after a protracted struggle by the Palestinain Arab citizens of the state for close to a decade, that its name was altered to the "General Federation of Workers in the Land of Israel" and thus Arab membership in Israel's trade union federation was made possible, though the aims and the constitution of the Histadrut remained essentially unaltered (see Davis 1977: 49-50; 91-103).

A brief review of the various important Zionist funding agencies will reveal a similar consistency. One of the first Zionist funds was the Fund of Preparation, established in 1918 and renamed in July 1919 the Fund of Redemption. This was the major fund underwriting the activities of the World Zionist Federation from 1918 until the establishment of the Foundation Fund in 1921. Over this period, the income of the Fund of Redemption totalled approximately one million pounds and was earmarked exclusively for the promotion of the interests of the Jewish community in Palestine within the framework of the World Zionist Organization (Talmi 1977: 340).

The Foundation Fund or the United Appeal for Israel was established in 1920 and registered in England in 1921. Until the establishment of the state of Israel, it acted as the financial arm of the "state in the making", underwriting Jewish immigration, absorption, settlement and defence in Palestine. It has since become the central financial agency of the World Zionist Organisation (Talmi 1977). The major land purchasing arm of the Zionist movement is the Jewish National Fund.

The JNF was established at the initiative of Professor Zvi Herman Shapira following an appropriate resolution taken by the fifth Zionist Congress in 1901. Its primary object is to:

> purchase, take on, lease, or in exchange, or otherwise acquire any lands, forests, rights of possession, and other rights, easements, and other immovable property in the prescribed region (which expression shall in this memorandum mean Palestine, Syria, any other parts of Turkey in Asia and in the Peninsula of Sinai) or any part thereof for the purpose of settling Jews on such lands. (Article III, subclause I, of Articles of Association of the JNF as registered in 1907 in England)

In 1954 an Israeli registered JNF company was established whose primary object was defined in very similar terms:

> To purchase, acquire on lease or in exchange, or receive on lease or otherwise lands, forests, rights of possession, easements, and any similar rights, as well as immovable properties of any class in the prescribed region (whose expression shall in this memorandum mean the State of Israel and any area within the jurisdiction of the government of Israel) or in any part thereof, for the purpose of settling Jews on such lands and properties. (Article 3a)

Prior to the establishment of the state of Israel, land was purchased on behalf of the Jewish people by the Keren Kayemeth Leisrael (Jewish National Fund). The JNF was established: "For the purpose of settling Jews in the prescribed region", to use funds in ways which "shall in the opinion of the Association be directly or indirectly beneficial to persons of Jewish religion, race, or origin". Lands owned by the JNF are exclusively for Jewish use. These lands "shall not be transferred either by sale or in any other manner . . . non-Jewish labour cannot be employed on these lands." (Chomsky, as quoted in Davis, Mack and Yuval-Davis 1975: 385; see also Davis and Lehn 1978: 3-33)

In 1961 the Israeli government concluded a covenant with the JNF endorsed by Parliament whereby the JNF is granted exclusive rights of administration and development of all State Domain Lands. In other words, the state commissioned a private organization, which is concerned according to its constitution with the promotion of exclusively Jewish interests in Palestine, to administer state lands although these should technically be utilized for the benefit of all its citizens, Jews as well as Arabs. These state lands technically constitute 75% of pre-1967 Israel. In addition, 14% of the lands in pre-1967 Israel are owned directly by the JNF — the remaining 11% are under private ownership. Thus non-Jewish citizens of the state of Israel — largely Palestinian Arabs who constitute some 16% of the pre-1967 Israeli population — are effectively and legally excluded from the right of purchase, lease, or any other requisition of rights of possession or other rights in 89% of the lands in pre-1967 Israel (Chomsky, in Davis, Mack and Yuval-Davis 1975; Davis and Lehn 1978).

It is in order to illustrate this seemingly abstract point by concrete example. On 23 March 1976, the director-general of the JNF, Shimon Ben-Shemesh, was interviewed by Radio Israel. He made an extensive statement which was reported as follows:

> During the past year, the JNF purchased lands in the territories for the sum of over 50 million [Israeli pounds, at that time about $6.6 million]. Among others, all the lands in the Nabi Samuel area were purchased, as well as huge tracts in the region between Ramallah and Latrun. According to the JNF Director-General, Shimon Ben-Shemesh, a Jordanian law stipulates the death penalty for Arabs caught selling land to Israelis. Nevertheless, there is today a large number of Arabs who wish to sell their lands to the JNF.
>
> Shimon Ben-Shemesh believes that the Arabs in the West Bank know that the JNF is purchasing land at market prices, and there is no shortage of sellers. On the contrary, a new institution has recently been developing: Arab middlemen and intermediaries, who provide the link between the sellers and the JNF.
>
> The major factor which influences Arabs and institutions to sell their land to Jews is the complete secrecy under which the transactions are carried out. Since the death penalty awaits every seller of land, the JNF has been careful: to this day, not even a single seller's name has been made public. The Director-General of the JNF says that decisions about the purchase of land are made by a committee of two: the Director-General of the Israeli Lands Administration, Meir Zore'q, and the Director-General of the JNF, Shimon Ben-Shemesh.

Information concerning lands available for purchase reaches the committee through a private intelligence service, as the JNF Director-General calls it. This private intelligence service is spread throughout various countries in the world; it can guarantee to sellers payment in any country and any currency: Argentinian pesos, French francs, or American dollars.

Most of the lands purchased during the last year are located in the area between Ramallah and the southern Hebron mountains, Ben-Shemesh said. We have purchased [square] meters, single dunums, and hundreds of dunums. We have purchased buildings, public institutions, and church property. Many of the Arab residents living on these lands are not yet aware that the lands are already owned by the JNF.

A substantial number of the owners of these lands live abroad, and the transactions were effected in their place of residence. The lands are purchased by the Hemnutah Co., founded by the JNF and the Israel Lands Administration. On lands purchased in rocky areas, the JNF plants forests and thus validates its ownership rights . . .

Shimon Ben-Shemesh explains that the JNF Board of Directors has decided that there will be no financial limitations placed on the purchase of lands, and that the JNF will continue the purchase of lands for the people of Israel, as heretofore . . . in any place, at any price, and of every size. (Transcript of Radio Israel news bulletin, 23 March 1976 [cited in Shulamit Aloni, "Is It Under Cover That We Should Purchase land?" *Yediot Aharonot*, 26 March 1976] quoted in Davis and Lehn 1978)

5. The Consciousness of the Conflict

The Palestinian-Israeli conflict has caused the death of thousands of human beings on both sides, and transformed the Middle East into an area of instability and continuous tension. It is not surprising, therefore, that the history of this conflict occupies a large portion of children's and young people's literature written and published in Israel for the Hebrew Israeli-Jewish readership. The basic feature that impresses me after reading this literature is that the problem is essentially presented as a "non-problem". It is represented in a radically one-sided manner: the Arabs are guilty of everything that has happened, or that will ever happen. They are not ready to understand the hearts and minds of the Jews. They are simply jealous of the Jews: therefore they began to attack them and raid their settlements, kill them and steal their property.

The Arab is portrayed in most of the books reviewed as a "foreigner". This essential "foreignness" of the Arab aims to prove to the young Israeli-Jewish reader that the Arabs, who are "foreigners", have no rights to the land. This "foreignness" of the Arab is also utilized to prepare the ground for a deeper explanation, which says that the Arabs, since they are "foreigners", came to the land in order to destroy it, and to kill and steal.

The portrayal of the Arabs as "foreigners" evolves from the notion that the land was uninhabited and desolate, that the Jews alone transformed it and made it flower:

> Joseph and his men crossed the country and came to the Galilee. They climbed the mountains, which were very pretty, but were empty. Joseph said: "Here we shall build up the Kibbutz, and here we will conquer the emptiness. And this place is Tel Hai . . . This is the land of wilderness, only mountains and mountains around, and silence. Here King David lectured, slept, and never arose. . . Empty is the land; it was deserted by its children; they are scattered and they do not take care of it; there is no one to guard it and no one to protect it. (Gurvitz and Navon 1953: 128, 132, 134)

The children's literature reviewed emphasizes at all times that Palestine belongs to the Jews: therefore when the Jews come to Palestine they are returning to their land which was deserted and virgin. All symbolic indications in the literature testify to the effect that Palestine was uninhabited and that it was waiting for the Jews:

> When he went up the hill he noticed large rocks which conspicuously were seen from the land. He examined them very carefully and then found part of several engravings. Evidently there was here an old settlement, he thought happily — and maybe the settlement was Jewish . . . We must stick here a peg and renew the old settlement.
>
> "Eitan," he called the youngster who had just returned from the fountain riding a horse and holding a pail of water. "Here on that hill, we will settle. Do you see these rocks? They are the remnants of an old settlement. Come and let us gather more rocks and lay the foundation of our new settlement . . ." (Semoli 1953: 12)

The idea of establishing a new settlement on the ruins of an old one implies that this land, Palestine, was uninhabited for a period of 2,000 years. Although the author uses the word "maybe", he immediately makes the reader believe that the settlement was originally Jewish, was demolished, and then the Jews returned to rebuild it. In order to lead one to this conclusion the author writes:

> Hermoni who stood up and tied bedspreads on top of the standing columns, stopped his work and approached the hole that Eitan [his son] was digging. His face expressed amazement and curiosity. He bent himself and looked at the broken rock.
>
> "Yes, marble," he whispered. "Bring me the pick-axe, Eitan. . ." Hermoni picked up the pick-axe and hit the rock a few times. The rock was big. He laid down the pick-axe and grabbed a handful of dirt which was on the surface. Slowly, slowly reliefs and engravings were clearly visible on it.
>
> "Again one column crown," said Hermoni with curiosity, "and we will try to get it out . . ."
>
> With a pick-axe and a hoe they worked in rotation and dug deeper around the buried rock. The youngsters came and gazed in curiously, and without a question they began to clean the dust which piled up next to the hole and removed it.
>
> For over half an hour father and son laboured until they succeeded to pull the rock. It was a marble slab the size of a square yard, which was partially chipped. With trembling hands they scratched the dust which was stuck on it. Eitan washed it with water, and in front of their eyes, various engravings were seen and they were clearly written: A Menorah with long stalks, a cluster of grapes and pomegranate . . .
>
> For over an hour they stood and looked at the strange remnant, which had been buried hundreds or maybe thousands of years. Whose hands had engraved these engravings? What did this board decorate?
>
> "That is a Hanukkiyyah," said Oz, [the second] son, after a long silence. "We will keep the slab for Hanukkah.* (Semoli 1953: 14-15)

* *Hanukkiyyah* is the Jewish Feast of the Lights; *Hanukkiyyah* is the Hannukkah lamp (consisting of eight candles plus one service candle).

The discussion ends here. No further indication is needed to prove that the settlement which was once on this place was Jewish. The symbols engraved on the marble slab are Jewish symbols. After that observation it really does not matter if the marble is hundreds or thousands of years old. There is no doubt that such ideas made it easier for new settlers to obliterate any feelings of guilt they might have. The land had been uninhabited and archaeology proves that it belonged to the Jews. This quote also explains the Zionist claim that the land of Israel belongs to one people only — the Jewish people. For hundreds or thousands of years, no one had worked on the land; when the son was ploughing, he found in the simplest way historical proof.

Often the author tries to present the same idea but in an open-ended manner, by raising the question and leaving the reader to draw the conclusions. Or the author tries to present the idea through the thinking of a character in the story.

Abner is a youngster full of curiosity, and he sees many Arabs who have commercial contacts with his father. He also sees Arab children and hears adults talking about the Arabs and about Jewish problems. As a result, thoughts come to his mind, and many unanswered questions:

> And again Abner asked his father: "Father, is it true that the land of Israel is the land of the Jews? Do not Arabs live here too? Do they agree that it belongs to the Jews?"
>
> "We think," replied the father, "that there is room in the land for the Jews and for the Arabs."
>
> But Abner did not continue asking, although his mind was not at ease. Here is the Arab youth, for instance, who came with his father to sell straw. He might be thinking the same way: this is my land, and here are the Jews who came and bought the land from the effendi, and they are dressed up nice and eat good things, and they already are saying that it is their land. There is no doubt that this Arab boy, and his father too, hate the Jews. Had they ever complained to that Arab boy why the Jews were forced to come to the land of Israel? (Margalit 1959:15)

In fact the father never answers his son's question. The question is very clear: does the land of Israel belong to the Jews and do the Arabs agree to that? The father's answer is unclear and amounts to no answer. This leaves the impression that the land of Israel belongs to the Jews but the Arabs can live on it. Since the author wanted to give the answer through the boy he went even further and gave the Jewish boy the opportunity to read the Arab boy's mind. Abner comes to the conclusion that the Arab boy and his father both hate the Jews.

Israeli Jewish authors often utilize a Palestinian Arab character to explain to their child readers that Palestine indeed belongs to the Jews.

In *The People of the Beginning,* the author explains how the hero of the story and his son visit a bedouin tribe. They are welcomed very warmly, and are admitted to one of the tents where the tribe's elderly sit. They drink a cup of coffee and the conversation moves on to the subject of the land; the hero of the story says that he has decided to live in the neighbourhood: "The elderly exchanged glances, and then immediately added: 'Inshallah [if God wills it], Hawaha, Ahlan wa Sahlan [You are welcome]. This is not our land, we heard that it belongs to the Jews'." (Semoli 1953: 24).

In another book, *Hasambah in Border Ambushes,* the author includes a passage spoken by an Arab, who sees the solution of the Israeli-Palestinian problem as having the Palestinian Arabs live wherever they are now; this means in the other Arab countries, because there they are amongst their own people: "God promised the land of Israel to the Jews, and because they suffered a lot of trouble in a period of 2000 years of exile, therefore the promise has finally arrived . . ." (Mosinson n.d.: 87).

The convincing power of these quotes is the fact that they are spoken by Arabs from Palestine. In other words, the young reader will be convinced that Palestine belongs to the Jews alone: even the Arabs say so.

There are some authors who do not conceal the fact that the Arabs truly lived in Palestine, but they say very plainly that the Arabs are strangers to this land, and since the land does not belong to them they did not do anything to develop it:

> The Arabs, who captured our land already before one thousand and three hundred years, did actually settle on it and they saw it as their country, but they did not do anything to protect it from destruction and ruin . . . While our land is occupied by strangers, it is becoming an empty land. The scattered of Israel lived in the lands of their exile and their eyes were anxious to return to their precious land. (Danni 1958: 13-14)

Here the author hopes to explain the fact that the Arabs who were in the land did not develop it and did nothing to rebuild the ruined cities; this apparently proves that it does not belong to them.

Throughout the literature there is repeated emphasis that the Jews are returning to Palestine (the land of Israel) after thousands of years of wandering:

> "Here it is," our teacher remarked. "Look children, and listen very carefully. In 70 diasporas our people were scattered during two thousand years of wandering. From one country to the other we wandered looking for refuge, like birds victimized by a storm. But now we arrived to safe shores. We returned to the land that we left thousands of years ago. Always we kept our eyes toward this direction, to Zion, our homeland. How delighted we are to see the return of Zion . . . We are newcomers from twelve countries in the class, and we talk several different and distant languages, but we have one dream and aspiration which brought us here, to the creation of Israel and the redemption of the old land. So stretch hands one to the other and be one body. Here we will materialize the three bases for our revival: one nation, one land, and one language. . ." (Semoli 1972: 23)

Here there is emphasis on the concept of "our land" and "our country". There is not the least mention of the fact that there is a partner in this land.

Occasionally the author may attempt to present a challenge to this position. Jum'a is a Palestinian youth who infiltrates his country after being expelled from it. He is captured by Israeli patrols. A Jew who knew him and his family sometime before the creation of the state of Israel meets him in jail. An argument develops where Jum'a tries to explain to "Hawaja Baruch" why he infiltrated into Israel:

> Jum'a was silent and I stopped my words. He is right and we are right too. We did not expel them, but they were expelled. What can I say to him? Shall I tell him about our Holocaust? About the destruction of our exile? Shall I tell him about our daring exodus, about the camps — concentration and death . . . About millions of Jewish immigrants. (Halevi 1971: 148)

The narrator seems to have been pushed into a corner. He is not able to convince Jum'a, whom he had known long before he (Jum'a) was expelled from the land where his family had once been master, and sent to live in a refugee camp where he is supported by the United Nations Relief and Works Agency (UNRWA).

"Hawaja Baruch" attempts to assuage his and the young reader's conscience with the argument that they (the Jews) did not expel the Palestinian Arabs, but that the latter "were expelled". Yet he appeals very forcefully to the Palestinian youth to understand the Jews and their suffering in the series of questions that he presents to the reader about the Holocaust, death camps and millions of refugees. He wants the reader to feel sorry for the Jew in order to justify the Zionist plan. He did not expel the Arab, and the homeless Arab refugee is obliged to understand him.

Even the seemingly liberal "Hawaja Baruch" does not recognize the fact that Palestine belongs to Jum'a. The end of the story is very abrupt. It ends when two infiltrators, Jum'a and his friend, are taken to interrogation.

> "So, listen to my advice," [said Baruch to Jum'a]. "Answer all the questions they ask you, and tell your friend to do likewise. I will stand on your side, and you will see that your punishment will be meted out as much as possible. . ."
>
> After that, Baruch finished his story. The interrogation ran smoothly. And this is what I tell you about the interrogation of the infiltrators. . . (Halevi 1971: 150)

An Arab who returns to his country must be punished. The Jew is welcomed with open arms. This is the message. The reason is that the land of Israel is claimed to belong to the Jews.

It is clearly difficult for the authors of the literature reviewed to explain to their child readers that there are Arabs in the "Land of Israel" who claim that it is their land.

The Zionist movement fell into the same trap. It was very important that the Jews and non-Jews believe that Palestine was uninhabited. It is interesting to note that although Zionist advocacy utilized religious and pseudo-religious claims, the religious element is missing in the children's books reviewed for this study. The argument that "God gave the land of Israel to the Jews" is not presented in a direct way. Secularism is dominant over religious sentiment. It is clear from the literature reviewed that the authors aimed to promote a secular point of view. The following extract illustrates how even a Jewish child does not know how a Jew prays.

> The Reddish carpenter withdrew some distance to a corner behind a group of trees. He wrapped himself with a praying shawl and prayed the morning prayer. Amalia noticed him and she gazed at him with surprise. "What is this father?" she asked with glittering eyes.
> "He is praying," answered Hermoni gravely.
> Eitan also approached the man and stared at him for a long time.
> "To God?" asked Amalia trembling.
> "To God," answered the father.
> "But why does he have this robe?" Hermoni and Zippor exchanged short glances. "It is the way Jews pray," Hermoni answered finally.
> "And why do we not have something like it?" Amalia asked. "Are we not Jews?"
> Zippor could hardly conceal his laughter and ran away. Hermoni was very embarrassed. (Semoli 1953: 93-4)

This secular frame of reference is typical of the children's story-books published in Israel until 1977, under Labour Zionist government. In 1977 Labour Zionism lost power to its long-standing rivals the Revisionist Zionist parties. Following this turning point, secular Zionist frames of reference both in official school curricula and in extra-curricular media of education were rapidly replaced with Zionist religious advocacy.

The concept of Zionism is explained to the young Jewish Hebrew reader as "making the desert bloom". The feeling is inculcated into the child that the land is his, not only from a historical perspective, but from a practical point of view: according to this philosophy it was only after the Jews converted Palestine into a "green and developing land" that the Arabs began to attack the Jews, in order to steal. This is how the majority of the writers explain the clashes between Jews and Arabs:

> The gloomy mountains gazed over the small camp of venturing pioneers, and the mountains were surprised and astonished. The Bedouins glanced with eyes full of hatred at those who crossed the borders of their country, and they started visiting them quite frequently. Upon sunrise they would infiltrate into the settlement to steal a cow or a calf. They would attack the ploughers in the field and steal the mules and display the people naked. They would even dare to enter into the homes, and take by strong hand, anything they wished or their hearts desired. (Semoli n.d.: 6-7)

> "The Arab thieves continued their ransacking and destruction," declared Elhanan, "and what the shelling failed to do, they are completing with their own hands. Every building of which some remnants are left is set on fire. God curse their memory." (Eliav 1975b: 15)

> From the north came the disaster, but in all other parts of the land Arabs began their conspiracies, stealing goods and murdering Jewish settlers. (Danni 1958: 82)

One of the most shocking descriptions I found in Y.Z. Schwartz's book, *The War of Independence:*

> Jaffa, the city of fanatics, infected by leprosy and whorehouses for foreign armies . . . [where] everybody intends to capture the neighbouring city of Tel Aviv, hopes to apportion the buildings and loot Jewish property . . . It was an hour of elation for the inhabitants of Jaffa, which further justified their profound time-honoured laziness. (Schwartz 1950: 41)

Thus, it is explained to the child that there is no dispute, it is only that the Arabs want to steal, and kill Jews. As a result of this line of reasoning, the Jew appears innocent because all that he wanted was to build a settlement, plough the land and make the wilderness flower. This presentation appears very often in children's books written prior to the establishment of Israel, and in those written from a historical point of view about the time when the Jews started their migration to Palestine.

There is almost no explanation to children that these lands, cultivated by the Jews, belonged to the peasants who attacked the Jewish settlements. And as we outlined in the first part of this research, every time that the Zionists bought a piece of land, they were committed to expel the peasants who had cultivated it for many generations. " 'The Effendi sold my land . . . my land, to a Jewish Effendi, who had long hair.' 'What is his name?' 'One name I remember . . . Israel and I do not remember anymore'. 'Keren Kayemeth Leisrael (Jewish National Fund)' whispered Gad . . ." (Talmi 1954: 103).

The quote above illuminates clearly an aspect of the Palestinian Arab problem. The Palestinian peasant depicted in this quote is profoundly attached to the land from which he ekes his bread and livelihood; then the Arab effendi, the owner of the land, comes and sells it to the Jewish effendi. In the eyes of the Palestinian Arab peasant they are identical, they are both "effendis". All that the peasant feels is that he is at the receiving end, the loser. He does not consider the transaction from the legal point of view; he is concerned that he is about to lose the source of his livelihood; he feels that the land is his. The author quotes the Palestinian Arab peasant as referring to the land as "my land" but she, of course, does not offer any explanation.

The main blame for the sale of the land and for the misery of the Palestinian Arab peasant is ascribed to the mysterious Arab effendi, who sold the land to the Jewish National Fund. The young Israeli Jewish reader is thereby absolved from any guilt. It is the Arab who is to blame. It is the Arab who is responsible for the fate of the Palestinian Arab peasant. It is the Arab effendi who betrayed a complete lack of concern for the fate of his peasant brothers. The Jewish National Fund, needless to say, did not commit any injustice to anyone.

When the Arabs in Palestine realized that Jewish immigration to Palestine was going to result in their dispossession, they started to organize against this immigration, land sale and the expulsion of farmers. At the same time the Jewish National Fund (Keren Kayemeth Leisrael) became very active, especially in the expulsion of the Arabs from their lands (Lehan 1974: 95-6).

The children's literature only explains these disturbances and revolts by saying that some Arab gangs took up arms to fight the Jews. Even before the Jewish immigrants arrived in Palestine, they would have heard about the "gangs" of Arabs who only attacked Jews:

> If at the beginning of the attack Tommy did not know who was the Jewish side, now he knows it very clearly. He was convinced that the attackers belonged to one of the Arab gangs. Even when he was on the ship they talked about their cruelty a lot. It was not hard for Tommy to come to this conclusion. (Yaffeh n.d.: 40-1)

After the expression "gangs" a new expression is used, "mobs", so the Jews will know whom they are fighting: "It was not very hard for Tommy to come to this conclusion" that the attacker was an Arab; "As a well trained partisan he knew that mob gangs lack discipline and fighters' cameraderie, and they would leave wounded members behind in the battlefield" (Yefet n.d.: 40-1). Thus, according to this literature, the root of the problem was that the Arabs, who are thieves, robbers and members of gangs and mobs, have no objective but to harm the Jews who returned to live in peace in the land of their fathers. Such descriptions abound in stories which tell of the "disturbances" before the establishment of the state of Israel in 1948.

The majority of the writers also emphasize the "evil origin" of the Arab agitators. For example, it is always claimed that the Palestinian Arabs actually accepted the fact that their land belonged to the Jews, but fought against Zionist settlement because of agitation by some fanatic and jealous Arabs who had no other objectives:

> At the beginning of May 1921, some Arab agitators with no consciences sparked an uncontrollable Arab mob in Jaffa. They told them lies about the Jews in Tel Aviv, and awakened them to attack their Jewish neighbours and inflict heavy damages on them. Hundreds of porters, shipyard workers and irreverent, hot-minded profit-chasers and blood-thirsty men took knives and wrenches in their hands. On a balmy spring morning they all jumped on the border neighbourhoods of Tel-Aviv-Jaffa. (Semoli 1972. 127)

What were the lies that were told to the Arabs of Jaffa? No explanation is given. Who were the Arab agitators? No explanation, since every Arab is potentially an agitator. Why did they do it? Because they are bloodthirsty.

> Suddenly a shudder passed through all passengers. Masses of hooligans, excited and agitated stood on both sides of the street, carrying in their hands sticks, rocks and knives, and with loud voices of contempt and the fever of murder they began throwing rocks inside the cars. (Eliav 1975b; 28)

During these days many foreign guests began visiting us. First they whispered with individuals, young and old, and later on they gathered all the village children in my Lord's house [the house which belonged to the owner of the horse who is telling the story]. They then agitated them and enticed them to attack the new settlers who were in the valley, and inflict injuries on them. Many youngsters followed them including young people from my Lord's family. (Bar-Adon 1966: 9)

Even here the whole story is mysterious. Who were these strange guests? Could it be that they were the organizers of the Arab protest in Palestine? And again they asked them to attack the Jewish settlers. There is no explanation of the background of the conflict. The narrator talks about agitation and excitement, not about ideologically and politically rational motivation:

The Arabs burst in their assault from the hills surrounding the kibbutz from the north and from the north-west. They charged at the kibbutz with untamed screams with no plan or order. These were not soldiers, they were only villagers who were excited and agitated. (Gal 1958: 96)

Other writers portrayed the subject of incitement in a different way. They wanted to demonstrate to the young reader that there were Arabs who did not respond to the incitement because they saw the "civilisation" that the Jews brought with them to Palestine.

All of the talk of the instigators in condemnation of the Jews fails to penetrate their ears. From the top of the mountain they see marshy lands which are transformed into a human settlement, and they cannot contain their admiration at the daring and ability and work and ambition. (Shaham 1959: 72)

Yet the authors were unable to conceal completely the fact that the Arabs were fighters, not only attackers: "Jerusalem was surrounded with war hungry Arabs, but on the way to Jerusalem there lay hostile Arabs in ambush. We only had few weapons and armoured cars in those days" (Zorea 1953: 24).

Some writers did attempt as rare exceptions to present the Arab's point of view as ideological. Yet, it seems that in none of these cases could the writers properly face the challenge, as the following paragraph illustrates:

Salim is a young Arab from the neighbouring village, and Gadi likes Salim. They spend many hours together between the branches of the mulberry trees which are in the Arab orchard . . . That day, the day of the big fire in the thicket, Gad was waiting for Salim. He asked him to tell him a story and to hear his opinion, but Salim did not come by. He wanted to go to the village, but they told him that it is forbidden to go. Also in the next morning Salim did not come. On the third day he came, and he stood next to the cactus stretch which divided the two villages and was very silent. Gad said to him: "Did you see the fire? The forest was in flames, why didn't you come to help?"

Salim answered sarcastically: "Why did you burn it?"

"Do you mean us, Salim?" asked Gad fearfully.

"And do you think that I am stupid? I don't know what they all know? You set the whole forest on fire."

"Lies, lies!" screamed Gad, and he couldn't control himself because of anger and sorrow.

"All of our village knows the whole truth," Salim was boasting, and he curved his body as though he was going to flee any minute.

"Shut up! Shut up you!" Gad hollered toward him. "Shut up and say why? Why grow trees to burn them? Why did we plant them?"

"Against us you planted, and against us you burned," roared Salim.

"Lies," said Gad . . .

"No lies. It is the truth. There is war Gad. There is a war."

"Why is there war? We do not want war."

"In our village they all know. Now everything is well-known. Before we were friends, and now I know that there will be war. Your tractors are devils, devils . . . We work with Allah, and you work with the devil. And he said that there will always be a war between Allah and the devil."

"Who said?"

And a very confused Salim answered: "There was an Effendi . . . from the large city."

Then Gad was silent.

Salim raised a large rock, Gad saw him, was afraid, and he also picked up a rock.

"Do you see this rock?" asked Salim. He waved it and tossed it in the field and after that he collected more rocks and tossed them in the field. They crossed the air with a whistle and fell in the ploughed area.

Salim then said: "Do you see, this is how the Jews will cover our fields, like these rocks. This is what he said [the Effendi] and he knows; he is from the big city . . ." (Talmi 1954: 124-5)

Again the author refers to outside instigation, through the mouth of the Arab boy. Several times the word "him" is used, but there is no explanation of who the outside effendi was or what he said. The boy was incited to act against his Jewish friend.

Regarding the 1948 war, we are told in the story that for the Arabs there was only one objective: to destroy the Jews. There is no explanation about national conflict or difference in points of view. Of course there is no talk about the objectives that the Jews worked for: the establishment of a Jewish state without Arabs. Therefore:

The war of Independence [1948 war] was the hardest war, the most desperate war, of the people of Israel in the last generations. The Jewish populaton in the land was 650,000 persons only against more than one million local Arabs, and more than 40 million Arabs in the neighbouring countries. The objectives of the one million Arabs who sat on the land was very awful and simple: to destroy in a blood bath and by butchery and torture all of the Hebrew inhabitants, and to ransack their homes and their property and to inherit the land, and to wipe all of the memories and those of us remaining out from under the skies and from the land . . . (Karmeli n.d.: 113)

The conflict developed, and after the 1948 war a large portion of the

Palestinian Arabs were expelled and thus became refugees in the neighbouring Arab countries. The problem of the Palestinian Arab refugees made the
political problem a humanitarian problem, too. Nevertheless, all the authors
reviewed predicate their presentation of the subject on the claim that the
Israelis "did not expel them". And when concerned they argue that "We did
not expel them, but they were expelled". (See above, p.61.)

In one story a Palestinian infiltrator was captured when he crossed into the
state of Israel. In his prison cell he meets a Jewish neighbour whom he knew
prior to 1948. The Jew is in a confused state of mind because he cannot dis-
avow the fact that the Arab is a native of that country, which is also his own
native land. On the other hand he is torn between himself and the Zionist
ideology, which calls for the establishment of a Jewish state:

> "I told you Hawaja Baruch," answered Jum'a . . . "We want to return to our
> homes and fields . . . often we climb the mountain overlooking our camp [the
> refugee camp] on our way to Irbid, and from the top of the mountain chain I
> can see the valley where I was born" . . . Hawaja Baruch answers: "Whatever
> happened to you is not our fault. You left Zemah of your own will. Nobody
> ever kicked you out, and your leaders incited you and scared you and called on
> you to leave. They are guilty of everything . . ." (Halevi 1971: 147-8)

Despite everything Baruch finds a way out. He tosses the guilt on to the
shoulders of the Arab leaders and thus solves the whole problem.
Nevertheless it does not help when Jum'a answers him: "I do not know whose
fault it was, but for us it is very bad, and now it is bad and bitter, because
between the upper stone and the lower stone of the mill the grains are ground
to dust . . ." (Halevi 1971: 148).

Despite his liberal thoughts, the writer could not solve the problem, and he
was forced to make an Arab say that the Arab leaders are the guilty ones: with
this the writer hopes that the conscience of the young reader will be relieved:

> Those who salvaged a little money built up a tent, but the majority of those
> [Palestinian refugees] were very poor peasants. They fled with a bundle of
> luggage and their livestock. Oh, we had a winter that only thanks to the
> blessings of Allah we did not all die. The help that our leaders promised to give
> us, never came of course. They announced that we were leaving the town for a
> couple of days and after the Arab armies demolished the Jews, we would
> return and burst into your villages and towns and would leave with a lot of
> property. That is it! They made a mistake and we paid the price in full. (Halevi
> 1971)

Sometimes the author tries to mislead his youthful readership in order to
prove his point. The following quote illustrates the attempt to prove to the
readers that it was the Arabs who did not want to live with the Jews:

> Everybody knows very well, and we [Israeli Jews] repeatedly and continuously
> state that this land is the land of the Arabs who were born in it, no less than our
> own land, the Israeli natives. But we *love it more than they do as a homeland*,
> because the Arabs have more lands which they see as their homeland, too, and

to which they are very faithful. . . But the Arabs do not want to live with us in brotherhood in our common country. Behind them there are millions of people, and they are very rich — more than all of the people of the world because they have plenty of oil. They also have strong allies, great powers, like Russia, China, France, England, and what have you. Therefore, even if they know very well that this land is our land no less than it is theirs, *or even more,* of our just right to live in it, especially when we agree to live in it in common with them, as equals in everything. . . They will not agree under any circumstances to accept our existence in our country, and they aspire in all ways and means to destroy us, as they destroyed a generation ago the Assyrians and the Armenians. . . But the Arab conspiracy to destroy us will not succeed, and why? Because *our quality and our human standards will be the decisive force* . . . We have noble objectives to live in our land as an example and a light to the Gentiles. (Karmeli n.d.: 106-8; emphases added)

If there were an Israeli government which were to declare that the Palestinian Arabs have the right to live in Palestine, and that the land belongs to the two peoples, then the Palestinian problem as we know it would not exist. But the author introduced these thoughts in order to attempt to prove to the young Hebrew reader by outright fabrication that the Arabs' only aim is to exterminate the Jews. He also found it suitable to differentiate between the Arabs' and the Jews' love for the country: "We love it more than they do as a homeland . . ."; "This land is our land no less than it is their land, or even more . . .". The purpose here is to convince the young Israeli Jew that "we" Jews always have more love and attachment to this land. Even though "we" want to live with the Arabs on this land, and even though we recognize it as their homeland, just as it is ours, the Arabs want to exterminate us. It is here that the author aims to introduce the notion of the superiority of the Jews over the Arabs. The Arabs will never conquer us, because "our quality and . . . human standards will be the decisive force".

Since the problem is presented, as I noted above, as "no problem", the authors of this children's literature take care to accentuate the fact that the Arab soldiers do not know why they are fighting and in fact do not want to fight. This point is emphasized in order to explain to the child the essence of the conflict, namely Arab jealousy of the Jew. The authors use statements by Arab soldiers to convey this idea. For instance, an Israeli Jewish boy crosses over to the Egyptian side in order to find out the position of the Egyptian front, and he meets an Egyptian soldier who does not identify him as a Jew. Then a dialogue develops as follows:

"And where are the rest of the soldiers?" asked Henriko, with tears in his eyes because of the sharp odour of onions. "They are playing cards. God wipe their names and their memories. They are idle and they do not want to work. By my life, I hate all of this fighting. Look and see: these Jews came to a desert and they made out of it a paradise, and here we come and convert that paradise to desert. By my life, we are nothing but jackasses. Eat, why do you not eat, o Muhammed [the phoney name of the Israeli boy]?" nagged Hasan [with] Henriko.

"I am not hungry. But why are you, Hasan, in the Egyptian army?" Henriko asked pointedly.

"They kidnapped me."

"What do you mean by 'kidnapping' you?"

"I came to Cairo to sell vegetables. I grow vegetables, and by all of the heads of cauliflower and cabbage that I have, I came to the market to sell my vegetables. Then the troops of the King, King Farouk, came by and they looked fattened like calfs, and they asked me to enter a car."

"Did you enter?"

"Me? No, no! But my legs entered before me. They stood up there pounding on my back, screaming at me, God have mercy on their sinful souls, and they whipped my back with straps. I did not enter — my legs entered first and I followed them . . . and away we go to Palestine, in order to fight the heathens. And what do I see? No heathens who besmirched the name of God, but cauliflower and cabbage growers like me," finished Hasan with a deep and heavy sigh. Mosinson 1975: 72-3)

When I examined how the problem between the Arabs and the Jews is explained and presented in children's literature, I came to the conclusion that the authors themselves did not find any problem or ideological differences or conflict of interests between the Arabs and the Jews in Palestine. The Jewish side is very well explained, and in the simplest manner. Palestine, which is the land of Israel, is the historical homeland of the Jews. There is no argument about the fact that it was a land desolate of any humans, other than a few nomadic bedouins who did not have a permanent home. This position explains the Zionist reference to "a land without a people, for a people without a land". The young reader is likely to accept these guidelines which will remove the feeling of guilt that the Arabs are trying to instil in him, namely, that Palestine belongs to them, and that they lived in it for generation after generation.

None of the books which refer to historical conditions in Palestine ever mentions the fact that the Arabs had established and built up cities and towns; that they had planted trees and orchards, and that the land was very green under their rule. Many books quote Herzl and other Zionist leaders, but there is not one book which quotes Ahad ha-Am who, following his visits to the country in 1891 and 1893, published a testimony to the effect, *inter alia,* that there was no single piece of cultivable land that had not already been ploughed and sown by others, namely the Arabs. But the authors do quote non-Jewish leaders, for example the German Kaiser who said that the land belonged to those who work on it (Semoli 1972: 159).

The authors cannot omit from their books and stories the fact that the Arabs began forcibly resisting the expropriation of their land, and demonstrating their objection to the Zionist project. Of course the authors do not explain the ideological differences or the incompatible political positions. They only tell the children that the Arabs were jealous of the Jews when they saw how rich and happy they were. They then began to steal from Jewish settlements and, when the Jews protested by force, the whole Arab population began using force.

The image of the Arab evolved from that of a thief to that of a murderer. The words "stealing" and "murder" are almost synonymous in most of the books which deal with these subjects. Arab political organization is called "conspiracy". The Arab does not think, therefore it must be easy to incite him. The disturbances which happened in Palestine are attributed in the children's books to the Arab leaders' incitement of their people who do not know exactly why they are told to object to the Jews. It is through these procedures that the authors remove any sense of guilt about the expulsion of the Arabs from Palestine, and place this guilt on to the Arab leaders. The Jews are thus completely absolved of responsibility for the destruction of Palestinian society. The Palestine tragedy is the responsibility of the Arab leaders, and ultimately, the responsibility of the victims, presumably for having the leadership that they deserve.

6. The Arab Character

In this chapter I intend to analyse how the character of the Arab is portrayed in the literature reviewed. My reading of the subject matter has brought me to conclude that the authors of the children's story-books covered by this study consistently present the Arabs in a most negative light. They make no distinction between those Arab characteristics which are produced by culture, specifically school, home environment and social norms, and those produced by situations of war and dispossession, expulsion and expropriation of the means of livelihood. The result is a very negative picture.

As far as I can see, the object of the authors reviewed in this study is to inculcate greater hatred of the Arabs in order to justify the political objective always promoted by the Zionist movement, namely the dispossession of the Arabs and the occupation of additional territory.

For instance, if the Arab steals, according to this literature, he must be fought and killed. Nowhere is there a discussion of his motives for stealing. If the Arab fights, he fights in order to murder people and he should therefore be killed. Nowhere is there a discussion of his motives for fighting. As a result, this literature tailors a very special character for the Arabs to suit the Zionist purpose.

Who Is the Arab?

There is no serious discussion in the literature of the question of who the Arab is. As a rule the young reader is left to make his or her own conclusions after finishing the book. In the few cases where there is a discussion of the question, it deals only with superficial details:

> Do you know who is the Arab? Abner knows. He knows that the Arabs rise early in the morning, perhaps even earlier than his father. It is interesting to watch them, to listen to the way they talk, because the Arabs are funny people.
>
> The Arab wears a dress and wraps a kerchief around his head like a woman. But sometimes he lifts his dress and puts something into his trousers and then one can see his black trousers. His trousers, like breeches, are only three-quarters length. They are very narrow at the ankles and very wide

between the legs; so large that one could put in there three large water melons.

When one wants to call an Arab, one shouts to him "Isma!" ("Listen!"), and when one talks with an Arab, he frequently repeats the word "Allah" or "hamdullillah". And there is a father's Arab and a mother's Arab.

What is an Arab child? Sometimes Abner saw in the street of the village Arab boys and even Arab girls. Abner noticed that all the Arab children always walk barefoot and they are dressed in all sorts of rags and tattered clothes. (Margalit 1959: 5-8)

The Arab presented here is anonymous and the description of him given by the author through Abner is stereotypical and reductionist. All Arabs rise early in the morning. All Arabs wear a dress and wrap a kerchief round their heads like a woman. All Arabs are funny people. When Arabs are called they are shouted at: "Isma". All Arab boys and girls walk barefoot and dress in rags.

The Arabs described here are non-specific; we are not told whether they are bedouin, peasants or city people. The purpose of this outline is to establish a stereotypical image of the Arab. For instance, the father explains to his son who enquires why the Arab children walk barefoot and dressed in rags as follows:

"There are also some who have much money, but they hoard their money and do not buy clothes and shoes. They also buy very little food; indeed you saw them satisfied with bread and olives or onions."

"If they have money, why don't they dress better? And why don't they eat properly?"

"This is what they are used to…" (Margalit 1959: 13-14)

The Thieving Arab

Thieving is presented in this literature as a typical Arab characteristic. The Arab is a thief by nature, but of course he steals only from Jews. I did not encounter a single book which presents an Arab stealing from another Arab. Thus, thieving is made a political act. The Arab thief is never identified as a specific person; rather, the literature defines the thief as an Arab. The literature does not attribute to the Arab thief any specific social motivation. We are not told whether the Arab thieves are rich or poor, or perhaps people who wish to become rich. The only specific motive which is sometimes raised is jealousy; the Arabs are jealous of the Jews with their wealth, happiness and good life, therefore they steal from the Jews. The Arab is always to be suspected of thieving. He can never be trusted. Consider the following extracts:

Throughout the years of my life in the land of Israel, I have come to the following conclusion (the narrator raised his voice): honour the Arab but also suspect him. (Semoli n.d.: 81)

"Watch them!" called father to Abner, as he turned home to fetch money to pay the Arab for the hay. Abner did not know what he had to guard.

"Abner, follow them up to the gate and see that they do not take anything," said father.

"Father, is it right that all Arabs are thieves?" asked Abner once.

"Who told you?" asked father amazed. "You should not talk like that." Father was embarrassed. "There are all sorts of Arabs," he said, "and among them, also thieves. It is impossible to know which Arab is a thief and which is not."

"Are there no Jewish thieves?" asked Abner.

"There are...not here...there are in the city. In our village, everybody is honest and no one will steal."

"But aren't the Arabs angry being watched as if they were thieves?"

"Perhaps they are angry, but what can you do?" (Margalit 1959: 11-14)

This dialogue is exceptional in that it deals with the question explicitly and the answers of the father are direct, not evasive. Yet even here the message is clear: true, not all Arabs are thieves but there is no way of knowing who is a thief; therefore all Arabs have to be watched. As for the Jews, there are Jewish thieves, but not here, only in the city. In other words, for the child any Arab he encounters is "maybe a thief" whereas in the context of the story he has no direct experience of Jewish thieves, since all the Jewish inhabitants of the village are honest people. And if the Arabs are angry — so what, let them be angry. The father, the author, the educator, clearly indicate that it is necessary to suspect every Arab of being a thief.

The question of stealing and its social significance in Arab society is presented in more sophisticated terms by Yirmiyahu Rabina through a long story relating to the Caliph Harun al-Rashid who employs a day thief and a night thief. The Caliph of course is very fond of his thieves and the story ends as follows:

Harun al-Rashid viewed them in silence and then indicated that they leave and take their departure. In their place he appointed his night thief as Mufti [supreme religious Muslim authority] and his day thief as Qadi (religious judge) in the capital of Baghdad, and their sons and their offspring as policemen and officers in all Arab states. The donkey was allocated a government allowance. And since then, the Mukhtar concluded his narrative and smiled at me, the seed of thieves among the judges of Arabia and its officers have continued without interruption and every donkey is given honour by the authorities until this very day. (Rabina 1948: 101)

This is a particularly interesting story because it is put into the mouth of an Arab, the Mukhtar, and deals with an exemplary and glorious period in Arab history. It attributes to Arab society features that make credible the appointment of thieves as the honoured and respected religious leaders, Mufti and Qadi, and makes their offspring policemen and officers, thus indicating that thieving is a deeply rooted feature of Arab society as a whole.

Throughout the literature reviewed for this study, I did not encounter any story which depicts the Jew as a thief apart from one solitary exception, Yigal Mosinson's *Hasambah and the Horse Robbers,* where a Jew working with a gang of robbers appears. I shall presently point out the important distinction between thieving and robbery as they are presented in this literature.

The Arab will take every opportunity to steal. He will even steal from the Holy Places: "When the legionaries saw that there was no-one in the monastery, they began to break the doors and cabinets searching for valuables. They destroyed and smashed as much as they could and then left the place" (Eliav 19756: 52).

Arab soldiers, when they occupy any locality, are concerned with nothing other than stealing and looting: "Other units of the legion roamed through the alleys, robbed and looted everything that remained there and then set the houses on fire" (Eliav 1975: 68).

This picture of the Arab as a thief is typical of almost all Hebrew children's books which deals with the social and political situation in Palestine both before and after the establishment of the state of Israel in 1948.

The Dirty Arab

Dirt, like thieving, is an integral part of Arab character in the literature under review. Dirt is typical of all aspects of Arab life and in the first instance it is typical of the Arab body:

> Their place was immediately taken by a gang of children and infants who walked about as naked as on the day of their birth: dirty, tangled hair and watery eyes. They surrounded them from all directions, their bellies large, swollen and protruding like full water bags. (Semoli 1953: 22)

Similarly, the young readers are also told that their elders and teachers regard Arabs as dirty. Thus, when a group of kids go with their teachers to see a bedouin camp, they are instructed as follows:

> "Children, do not go too close to them," called out the teacher Bat Sheva. "Look how dirty they are."
> Abner withdrew with embarrassment from the Arab boy [who had invited him to come in]. Indeed the boy looked very dirty: his clothes, his legs, his hands, his face, and flies walked all over him and he did not seem to notice. (Margalit 1959: 20)

Arab clothes are also dirty and stink. When this is pointed out to them, they seem to see nothing wrong with it — in fact they consider the stench to be good. One of the stories concentrates on Jewish children who are taken captive by Arabs and carried off to an Arab village.

> As they entered the village, they were enveloped with the smell of charcoal that is distinctive of Arab villages and which further intensified their dejection.
> They walked slowly along the road which was strewn with stones and animal dung, escorted by hordes of children of all ages, barefoot, filthy, dressed in rags, who ran around them from all directions with their mouths and their eyes wide open from curiosity and wonder. (Dominitz 1956: 25)

> The children dropped on the mat and pretended to fall asleep but it was cold. The tattered *'abaya* which served probably in its earlier incarnation as a cover

for a camel, covered with oil, emitted such a heavy stench that it was necessary to remove it to the adjacent room. The children lay in silence for a long time yet they were sleepless despite their great fatigue.

"It is terribly cold," grumbled Menachem. Shimshon got up and opened the door. The guards immediately jumped at him. "What happened? It is forbidden to go out."

"We are very cold," called Shimshon, "we cannot sleep."

"Were you not given something to cover yourselves with?" the guards exclaimed in surprise.

"There was an *'abaya,"* said Shimshon, "but it is so very…stinky. It is impossible to use it as a cover."

"Where is it?"

Shimshon brought the *'abaya* from the adjacent room; the Arabs examined it, smelled it and burst out laughing. "Indeed this used to cover a camel. This is a very excellent smell." One of them took off his own *'abaya* and gave it to Shimshon and covered himself with the *'abaya* that previously served as a cover for the camel. Also this garment did not emit the smell of distilled perfume, and Zvi, who was somewhat fastidious and very sensitive to smells, was one hundred percent certain that this *'abaya* also served in one of its previous distant incarnations the same respected use as the other *'abaya*. (Dominitz 1956: 30-1)

Not only are the clothes of the Arabs stinking and dirty, but also their homes. In all the books reviewed, I did not come across a single reference to clean Arab homes or clean Arab villages.

Naturally the result of physical filth is illness: a warning against getting too close to the Arabs and catching contagious diseases. In the following story, the exceptional circumstance is presented where a Jewish boy befriends an Arab boy who invites him for a visit. The mother of the Jewish boy does not prohibit the visit but neither does she fail to warn her son very sternly: "His mother warned him not to leave the tent camp of the Bedouin tribe, not to go on long excursions and to be careful not to contract the various diseases that are common within the tribe" (Burnstein-Lazar 1968: 19).

The Cursing Arab

One of the consistent and most marked features of Arab behaviour as portrayed in the children's books reviewed in this study is regular, intense cursing. These books, almost without exception, make constant cursing an attribute of the Arabs. When the Arab wishes to impress his audience, he must swear. The portrayal of the Arab in such terms is intended to reduce his dignity and demonstrate that he is not serious. The Arab curses everyone, including himself and his children. He cannot address his enemy or his subordinate without swearing, which makes any open dialogue or serious discussion impossible.

For instance, in one of Eliav's stories, Jewish children are taken captive by Arabs:

The two [boys] got up with their hands raised above their heads and walked towards the legionary who began laughing and glaring at them with looks that made them perspire. When they approached him he charged at them and began hitting them with the butt of his gun, screaming at them: "You sons of a bitch! I shall now pluck your heads off your shoulders!" (Eliav 1955: 14)

Similarly the attitude of an Egyptian army officer to his subordinates is expressed by the following address: "Dog son of a dog, the seed of miserable peasants (fallah)" (Mosinson 1975: 92).

Not only does the father curse his sons, but the son can be portrayed as cursing his father, one of the most extreme blasphemies in Arab society. In one of these stories, a situation is described where the Arab son and daughter rebel against their father, who wants to fight the Jews. The daughter falls in love with a Jewish man and the father goes out to kill his daughter and her lover. He fails, and is taken prisoner. His son turns to him and:

"You are a devil, not a father," grumbled Mahmud. "What wrong did Aziza [his sister] do? What wrong did I do? Why do we have to die? Just because of your stupidity and ignorance? You live like people lived thousands of years ago . . ." (Mosinson 1973: 155)

Or again, when a group of people who engage in smuggling travellers across the border between Jordan and Iraq are caught, they are addressed by the Iraqi officer as follows:

By all ghosts and devils, may your soul and your mother's soul be liquidated and may the prophet curse you and may you never be blessed to sit under the protection of his beard. Have you gone completely mad that you behave in such a thoughtless manner attempting to smuggle people across the border? (Eliav 1975a: 117)

And again in another of Eliav's stories, Jewish children are taken into captivity and subjected to abusive swearing:

"May the devil enter the spirit of the forefathers of the Jews; may the curse of the devil be visited upon them; may they be damned by the prophet for the rest of their days. There is no respite from their attacks." The armed man was cursing and shooting alternately, incessantly in all directions. (Eliav, 1975d: 88)

The Arab is presented as an expert at swearing:

When a little boy with forelocks and a skullcap on his head runs and slips and falls, he will immediately raise his holy book of studies which he carries and kiss it . . .
When a big Arab peasant chases a little boy who stole an apple off his basket and trips while running, falling full length flat on the slippery stones to the glee of all the children of the neighbourhood, he will immediately open his mouth and curse them in Arabic as well as their fathers and the God of the Jews. These Arabs are great experts in cursing and there is a special taste for an Arab curse. (Shahar 1961: 33)

Swearing by the Arab as presented in this literature is invariably used to hide weakness, to justify a lie, or to present the Arab as irrational. Thus the Arab loses dignity with his audience, for this literature a mainly Jewish audience, who invariably begin to smile when the Arab commences cursing. The Israeli Jewish authors elaborate extensively on the subject of swearing by Arabs and introduce the feature of Arab curses or even curses in Hebrew which do not have an Arabic equivalent into most of their stories and books.

The Corrupt Arab

Corruption is a part of the Arab way of life. This is the clear conclusion to be drawn throughout the literature in question. The Arab will sell anything and everything, including his soul. Consider, for instance, the following narrative: Two Jews who have been taken prisoner by Arabs establish contact with another Arab group which tries to use them for their own purposes. Yet the Jews pay them money to secure their assistance:

> "Are you not afraid that they might betray you one day?" asked Nissim anxiously.
> "This may very well happen, but so long as the general situation remains as it is and so long as I have much money at hand, there is nothing much to fear since these guys are willing to do anything for money, even sell their own mother." (Eliav 1975d: 89)

In this story by Eliav, a group of Arabs are given a sum of money to sink an Israeli ship. The group are thoroughly corrupt and, instead of executing the task themselves, they hire other people to do the job; "by coincidence", the people hired are Jews:

> Our employers [the Arab group] will receive a considerable sum of money for carrying out their designs, but being corrupt people they decided to carry out the task without exposing themselves to risk, therefore they chose us. This is exactly it my friend. They will send us to carry out the sabotage. Should we be successful, they will reap the fruits of our success as if they themselves carried out the task. But should we fail or get killed or get caught, they will always find some excuse to justify to those who sent them on the job why they sent us to carry out the task. In truth, our employers are fainthearted cowards of whose ilk there are very few. Of this I am convinced. In the end they will not have the courage to carry out their own designs themselves. (Eliav 1975d: 104-5)

In the book *The People of the Beginning,* an Arab character named Abu Ni'ma is presented in the most negative light: he is corrupt, motivated by greed, a filthy character. There are such people in every society, but the author throughout the book fails to present any positive Arab character to balance the negative impression projected by Abu Ni'ma. The young reader will be clearly impressed by the implication that all Arabs are corrupt. On the other hand the author describes in great detail how the Jewish hero refuses unequivocally to co-operate with the corrupt Arab, although the latter proposes a deal where he could make a lot of money. The picture is clear: the

Arab is corrupt whereas the Jew is free of corruption. The whole of Chapter Five of the book, 25 full pages, are devoted to this theme:

> "What is your monthly salary, Abu Eitan?" he [Abu Ni'ma] asked suddenly with a wink.
> "Six liras," answered Hermoni briefly.
> "That's little, Abu Eitan, that's little . . ." whistled Abu Ni'ma as if in compassion.
> "What can we do?" sighed Hermoni. "I and the members of my household will work here; we will plough and sow the lands and reap bread and vegetables from the land and Allah will help us . . ."
> "It is possible to live differently," said Abu Ni'ma with a wink, twirling his moustache. "The shepherds in the forest must pay grazing taxes for every head of sheep and cattle. They do not live in misery . . . Also charcoal is a lucrative business, Abu Eitan," added the visitor. "You could live here like the faithful live in paradise, rather than waste your strength in the despicable labour of peasants (fellahin). (Semoli 1953: 53)

The features noted above are only the most prominent Arab characteristics presented in the literature. As well as these there are subsidiary features such as flattery, cowardice and deceitfulness, but these are not as developed.

It is also clear that the image of the Arab is presented in such terms as to undermine any possible positive relationship between Jews and Arabs in Palestine. The young reader is educated through this literature to avoid the Arabs. He or she is warned not to approach the Arabs because they are physically filthy and diseased, because they steal, because they cannot be trusted, because they swear constantly, and because they are corrupt.

The Bedouins

Bedouins appear in a large proportion of this literature, especially in books dealing with the period prior to the establishment of the state of Israel in 1948. The image of the bedouin is given considerable attention in the literature because the bedouin, his story and his lifestyle, could be conveniently manipulated to cover up a number of key issues central to the life of the Zionist settlers in Palestine. The Zionist movement aimed to demonstrate that Palestine was uninhabited, yet it could not completely disregard the fact of the existence of the Palestinian people resident in the country. In an attempt to bridge this inconsistency, it developed, concentrated on, and expanded the image of the bedouin.

The first and most important issue which the authors of the literature under review wish to demonstrate is the lack of any connection between the Arab, the bedouin, and the land. The bedouin is a nomad who shifts from place to place. The central elements in his existence are water and pasture. He does not cultivate the land and therefore lacks any deep ties with it. Since the bedouin has no deep spiritual connection to the land he lacks any spiritual connection with his homeland. It is similarly alleged in this literature, and posited as a fundamental aspect of the bedouins, that they are indifferent to their country of residence and recognize no borders. Today, a bedouin could be resident in Palestine; tomorrow in Egypt; then in Jordan or Syria or any other locality that seems suitable or attractive at the time.

This central point is posited as proof of the correctness and justice of the principal slogan of Zionist advocacy since the establishment of the Zionist movement at the turn of the century: that Palestine was empty of population. It is of course true that there were Palestinian bedouin tribes in the land but it is clearly a flagrant distortion, in fact an outright lie, to reduce the existence of the Palestinian Arab population, with their dense village settlement and peasant cultivation, to bedouin existence.

Zionist advocacy was aided by the fact that the image of the bedouin was familiar in the West, especially in Europe, more so than any other Arab image or lifestyle. Around the turn of the century, the West came into close contact with bedouin tribes, bedouin politics and bedouin society in the Middle East, especially in Saudi Arabia where T.E. Lawrence organized bedouin alliances and mobilized bedouin assistance in the campaign against the Ottoman Empire in World War I. This made it relatively easy for Zionist advocacy to establish the Zionist case convincingly before Western public opinion. Also, given Western racialist categories which were developed in parallel with the expansion of Western imperialism, it was easy to underline the radical differences between the Jew and the bedouin. (See e.g. Said 1978; 1980.)

The Jew came to settle. He dressed as a European. His business was "civilization"; he engaged in productive work and was part of the all-embracing Western enterprise. The local bedouin could hardly compete with this image. These elements were not only central to Zionist advocacy in the West but are fundamental elements in the children's literature under review, essential to the development of a structure that could enable the Zionists to present in a convincing way the justice of their case, the "Jewish national liberation movement".

Generally in the literature, the authors attempt to imbue their child readers with the idea that the Arab is always essentially a bedouin. It is, therefore, a characteristic feature of this literature that the terms "Arab" and "bedouin" are used as synonyms and replace each other in any context as if every Arab was a bedouin.

The bedouin appears arbitrarily and suddenly, and disappears in the same way.

One day there appeared in the Valley of the Spring donkeys and camels laden with packets and parcels and accompanied by women and children. The men lowered the camels in a wide circle and unloaded the packs off their camels and donkeys. Within a short while, the tents were up and columns of smoke emerged out of the fires interspersed among the tents winding their way into the sky. Hermoni [the father] was at the time in the forest when Tiqvah [the mother] and the children went down to the Spring. The visitors received them with obvious surprise and watched them with open hatred. They sent their donkeys to feed on the clover field which Hermoni sowed near the Spring and the bedouin children penetrated into the vegetable garden and pulled out radishes and then robbed the first early crop of cucumbers. (Semoli 1953: 142-3)

Another example:

Ahmad forced his horse into a fast gallop. Soon the tree next to which the camp was put up appeared before him. But where had the tent disappeared? Ahmad could still see the holes in the ground which marked the places where the pillars of the tent were positioned. He saw a heap of amber and partly burned wood. Next to the heap of amber and partly burned wood, there was an old copper kettle and a number of broken wooden boards were scattered around the place where previously shelves to store the fruits and vegetables were fitted . . . But the tent, his uncles, his mother Hasana had all disappeared. (Feder 1964: 50-1)

The bedouin crosses borders unawares. He is completely indifferent to borders since he has no specific ties to any specific country.

Other passengers were sons of a Bedouin tribe in the Sinai. They said that they were attempting to travel north into the settled regions but that they did not like these regions at all and that they were therefore making their way back together with their sheep and donkeys to El Arish. (Naor 1974: 87)

Since the bedouin plays a central role in Hebrew children's literature, the authors make considerable efforts to present all aspects of bedouin lifestyle, custom and dress, rarely omitting any detail of significance. As noted above, this effort is made in the context of a clear attempt to demonstrate that the residents of Palestine were only bedouin.

The bedouin raise only black sheep, explained Nisi, who read extensively in the library of Mister Aron on Eretz Israel and its population, in order that he would be able to discern and distinguish the local population without difficulty even at a distance. (Nadel 1974: 97)

Note that the reference is to the land of Israel, that is Palestine, and all of its population, not to Palestine and some of its population, namely the bedouins.

In so far as bedouins' cleanliness is concerned, the image is uniform; the bedouins are presented as invariably filthy: "'Let us see how they live in their tents,' said Nadav contemptuously, 'filth and stinking manure'" (Margalit 1959: 18).

The bedouin is also portrayed as a thief:

Even the Arab shepherds who bring their herds to the spring to drink abstained from coming to the spring on these days [when foreign bedouin came to the place]. And when they met Hermoni in the woods they warned him to watch his farm very carefully . . . because these nomad Bedouins are like thieves. (Semoli 1953: 145)

Similarly, the bedouin is a robber:

"Aleihum! (attack them!)" a voice was sounded all of a sudden and already
strong arms held us tight forcing our hands behind our backs and two figures
dressed with black gowns appeared before us. The figures had long ponytails;
robber Bedouins. These were not the screams of fun, nor was it a child's game,
nor was it an imaginary scene. These were robbers, real robbers who took us
captive in order to levy ransom. (Chernowitz 1960: 127-8)

Almost every action taken by the bedouins in their everyday life and every
item of dress are described in detail in these children's stories. The tents are
described in detail. In one of the books reviewed, I found a description of a
bedouin *'abaya* and of why the *'abaya* is so central to bedouin life.

"The *'abaya* is an excellent dress" argued Nisi, defending very enthusiastically
the traditional dress of the Bedouin. "They are suitable dress for winter as well
as summer; for lying as well as sitting and walking. In the winter, the Bedouin
covers himself in the *'abaya* in which he can wrap himself almost twice and
keep himself warm. The *'abaya* also protects him against the rain. It is woven
very tightly and the grain of the wool faces downwards so that the rain is not
absorbed in the cloth but rather washes over it as if protected by oil. In
summer, the *abaya* insulates a thick layer of air between the folds of the *'abaya*
and the human body and this layer of air protects the body from the heat and
also prevents heavy sweating. One of the permanent fundamental fears of the
Bedouin who is the man of the desert is a shortage of water. The *'abaya*
protects the level of liquid in his body, although because of the lack of sweating
his body is not cooled by the sweat. The *'abaya* is very comfortable bedding at
night. In short, its advantages are too numerous to be counted." (Nadel 1974:
96-7)

What does a bedouin "camp" look like?

This is how the Bedouin camp looks from a distance. Black tents stretched
over barren land. The tents are made of sheets woven of camel's wool which
the Bedouin weave with their own hands. These sheets protect them from the
sun in the summer and the rain in the winter. There are tents of various sizes
and the size of the tent is related to the size of the family living in each tent. The
largest and most spacious tent is the tent of the sheikh. This tent is a kind of
Bedouin royal castle. Its floor is covered by very beautiful carpets and over the
carpets coloured silken pillows are heaped. In this tent the visitors are received
and there also the elders of the tribe convene for important sessions. (Benni
1958)

Most of the authors insist that there are no problems of any consequence
with the bedouin, largely because they have no land. The main problem in
relations with them is bedouin theft and occasionally killing. It is significant
that the bedouin is not generally characterized by "cruelty". Whenever a
cruel deed is presented, the bedouin is immediately replaced with an Arab. (I
shall elaborate on this below.) The bedouin is not presented as the real

enemy. In many of the stories, the bedouins often appear as sympathizers and supporters of the state of Israel: "Mohammad Ahmad al-Heib, the scout of the reconnaissance unit, was a medium-sized youth, rather unimpressive. He did not even cultivate a mustache which is a source of pride for every Arab" (Nadel 1974: 72). Mohammad, the hero of this story, serves in the Israeli army and captures three "terrorists".

> The adults [in the Kibbutz] believe that grave danger awaits any person who dares go outside the boundaries of their farm. They did not permit even a short walk. The youth often grumbled and protested against this regime especially since the Bedouins did not appear at all to be enemies and they came to the kibbutz often and regularly. Amnon explained to the children the reasons for these strict instructions. These instructions were imposed not because of the danger of the Bedouin who live in the Negev but because of the Arab states around. These states refuse to admit that the war is over and kept sending infiltrators against the border with the aim of murder and robbery inside Israel. They also attempted to incite the Bedouin against the Israelis and sometimes these attempts were successful; sometimes they failed. Most of the Bedouin tend to support the Israelis and detest the Arab warmongers. (Feder 1964: 66)

In all descriptions of the bedouins, special emphasis is placed on their folklore and dress: *hatta* (traditional Arab men's headdress); *'aqal* (headband to keep *hatta* in place), and *'abaya;* (cape worn by bedouin); their tents and their customs. There is no mention whatsoever of their social or political thought. The only political elements mentioned are either that they are incited against Israel by the Arab states, or that they are faithful to the state of Israel, with no real explanation of why this should be the case. They appear as people who are not aware of what is happening around them and do not really care. Their national origin is mentioned only in association with acts of theft or atrocities. Only then is the bedouin given a national identity: Arab.

Generally, compared to the image of the non-bedouin Arab, especially after the establishment of the state of Israel, the bedouin is presented in positive terms. The reason for this is clearly political: the authors of the literature under review wish to demonstrate that Jewish society and the state of Israel are not in real conflict with the bedouins who have no lands and therefore cannot clash with the ideology and practice of Jewish settlement in Palestine. It is largely for this reason that pre-1948 Arab society is reduced to bedouin society throughout the literature.

The Image of the Positive Arab

In most of the books reviewed in this study, there appears the character of the "positive Arab" — positive from a Zionist point of view. This cannot be sufficiently emphasized. All instances of the positive Arab as portrayed in the literature refer to an Arab who wittingly or unwittingly has come to accept the

Zionist point of view on Palestine. The positive Arab is portrayed as the ideal Arab of the future. The efforts to portray this image as human and dignified invariably collapse because they are based on an essential contradiction. For an Arab to qualify as a positive Arab he must violate his sense of integrity and dignity, and collaborate with the Zionists against his own leadership and his own people.

The contradiction comes into sharp focus if examined against the image of the positive Jew. Whereas the positive Jew fights for his people and his country, the positive Arab refuses to fight; the positive Jew collects information, the positive Arab passes information.

Invariably, the positive Arab is devoid of national and political values. Such characters are classified as traitors by their people. It may be that this image can elicit the sympathy of the young Hebrew reader; it is doubtful that it would elicit his or her respect. We have already quoted from Yehudah Salu's *Fire in the Mountains*. The book tells the story of a group of children who embarked upon a campaign to "liberate Jerusalem". The group is taken captive by "an Arab ambush" on the approaches to Jerusalem. The hero of the story is wounded and attempts to escape and reach a Hebrew settlement. He is saved by a "positive Arab" named Ali. The character of Ali is juxtaposed with that of his cousin Husni:

> "This is Husni, my cousin. Here he is a big commander."
> "He looks a lot like you, almost as if you were twins."
> "Yes, he looks a lot like me, but only his face, not his soul. He has a black soul." (Salu 1970: 34)

Husni is a fighter for his people. In other words, he is a "gangster" and a "robber". He is portrayed in a negative light, to underline the positive character of Ali who harbours the Jewish child, refuses to fight and considers the Palestinian fighters to be "low murderers".

How did Ali come to his position of positive Arab? How did he come to see the light? Here is Ali's story:

> After some time I met a Jewish young man, a very good young man who lived near the Schneller school. His name was Gershon. He taught me to read and write Arabic [sic]. He had many pupils and in the evenings we would assemble in his rooms. It was Gershon who taught me my way of life. He used to tell me: Ali, I do not want you to become a Jew, I want you to remain faithful to your people, but first of all be a human being because that is the main thing. He used to say that the world is large and that everyone has a place in the world and that every human being if he labours honestly will find a dignified livelihood. He used to say that all the troubles originate because of people who do not wish to work but only exploit and cheat their brethren. They incite hatred among the people and cause wars and bloodshed.
>
> I knew Gershon for one and a half years. He was for me both a teacher and a friend. Then came the riots and Gershon was killed in these mountains. More than ten years have passed since then. After Gershon died I remained like a ship without a wheel; I did not know what to do . . . Here away from the city I

wanted to establish an Arab Ben Shemen [agricultural/vocational school].

I always thought that this is the thing that we the Arabs need too: a school where the youth will study the Arts and the Sciences, vocational crafts, agriculture, but in the first instance will be educated to be human beings. (Salu 1970: 42-3)

This narrative is deeply illuminating. Seemingly Ali gained a great deal from his friendship with Gershon. Gershon made him literate and showed him his way in life, yet their relationship was fundamentally asymmetrical: Gershon was killed while fighting for his ideal, namely the Zionist ideal of establishing a Jewish state, whereas Ali's political consciousness and will were emasculated by his relationship with Gershon and he is not willing to fight for his homeland.

Similarly, Ali wants to establish an agricultural school like the Ben Shemen Zionist establishment where the pupils will learn "Arts and the Sciences, vocational crafts, agriculture, but in the first instance will be educated to be human beings". There is, of course, a crucial fallacy in his position. Ben Shemen was in the first instance a fortress of Zionist education and a fighting position in the pioneer frontline. Ben Shemen pupils were not educated in the first instance to be human beings but rather to be fighters committed to the cause of Zionism and the establishment of the Zionist state. Had Ali hoped to introduce the complete model of Ben Shemen in the service of the cause of Palestine he would not be presented as a positive Arab. It is because he came to adopt a politically emasculated image of Ben Shemen that he could be trusted by the Jewish boy hero:

Ali's voice quivered with excitement. At last he had found an opportunity to open his heart, if only before a youth like myself. I now knew he would be a faithful friend and I could trust him with all my heart. He would not betray me nor deliver me into the hands of the gang of murderers which established itself in Deir Ammar. (Salu 1970: 43)

In the following, the Jewish hero further reduces the person of Ali: "Had there been many like yourself among the Arabs this war would not have been visited upon us . . . I forgot that I came to this place in order to take part in the fighting" (Salu 1970: 45). Needless to say, it was Ali's political emasculation that made it possible for the young Jewish hero to forget the circumstances of his arrival in the place.

A similar picture of the positive Arab is presented by Eliezer Semoli in *The Sons of the First Rain*. Jewish schoolchildren are taken to visit an Arab school. The Arab school is very backward. The pupils are seated on the floor, the classroom has only one window just under the ceiling which hardly allows any light in. The pupils are dirty and the teacher walks about with a whip. At some stage later the Arab teacher decides to reciprocate the visit. The Jewish teacher suggests showing them the school and "what the Jews are doing in the Land of Israel". Of course the teacher and pupils are amazed and deeply impressed by the facilities, the classrooms, the cleanliness, the workshops, etc. The Arab teacher develops into the "positive Arab" character in the story. Here is his statement:

"In the name of God there are many things we have to learn from you, the Jews. This place was barren and deserted and you came and through your energy, you transformed it into paradise, vegetables, flowers, shade-giving trees. There are numerous such plots even larger than this in our village and they serve as lair to donkeys and camels without anyone growing anything on them.

"Behold, the bountiful water you have here and how good it tastes. I read daily in the papers advocacy of hatred against the Jews. Many in this country are inciting and instigating feuds between our sons and your sons, but as I pass through your streets and witness the huge labour that you invested in barren and deserted sand hills which you transform into blooming gardens, I always say in my heart: God sent the Jews here to serve as an example for us. We shall observe them and do the same. The main thing is that we live in peace as good neighbours. Here you paid us a visit and also we came to see you at your school.

"Let our hearts draw close and the hatred end. In what have we sinned and what shall we gain by feuds and quarrels? For hundreds of years the country was under Ottoman rule and now it awakes into blessing. We have obtained through you better welfare. We have benefitted from your capital, your energy and your good example.

"Let us aspire therefore" — he turned to our teacher and shook his hand — "that our children after us will understand each other and work together for the welfare of the country as a whole." (Salu 1970: 141)

Another aspect of the good Arab is portrayed through the wise old native who represents reconciliation to the Zionist point of view:

Do you know, O children, do you know, good boys, why is it that we all fled away? We fled away from the war with the Jews. And why did this cursed war begin? Who is responsible that this cursed war broke out? Not our peasants (*fallahin*) are to blame but in the name of Allah the merciful, Abd al-Qadir is to blame. May the Lord destroy the home of Abd al-Qadir and the curse of Allah be upon his head because he was the one who became commander and brought his *Mujahidin* (freedom fighters) to our mountains and our villages al-Jaba, Beit Natif, Surrif, Bab al-Wad and al-Quds, and this is what he said:

"O *Fallahin,* the renowned sons of Arabia, the Jews want to rob our lands, loot our homes and take our daughters. We will butcher the Jews and remove them from Palestine and there will be no more Jews in Palestine."

The peasants, the sons of the villages, heard the statements of Abd al-Qadir and believed him. They left the ploughshare, the horse and the donkey, deserted the vineyard and the wheat in the field and followed him. They joined the *Mujahidin* of Abd al-Qadir . . . they were heroes, the young men of the Jews, they were very courageous heroes, O my children. (Weinberg 1956: 140-2)

The Arab who says this is presented as a wise man who sees and understands the truth. Abd al-Qadir al-Husseini was one of the most important Palestinian Arab commanders in 1948 and is universally recognized as a great historical person. This is why the author found it necessary to attribute the above quote to the old and therefore wise Arab. A "positive" old and wise Arab character appears regularly in the literature reviewed. A wise Arab is an Arab who sees the truth of Zionism and accepts the fact that Palestine belongs to the Jews: "the old man exchanged glances and then added with a slight bow: 'May this be God's will. O master, welcome. This is not our land. We heard that it belongs to the Jews' " (Semoli 1953: 24)

Likewise, the literature knows how to depict the positive character of an Arab soldier. This is of course a soldier who is reluctant to fight and is ready to betray his people. Thus in one of the stories we read of an Israeli youth who crosses the border into Egypt in order to spy and find out when the Egyptians are planning to attack Israel. He is caught by a dissatisfied Egyptian soldier who tells him that he came to this place not in order to fight but because he was taken under the threat of force. The Egyptian soldier soon understands that the boy is a Jewish spy, but then what happens?

> Henriko [the young Israeli spy] shuddered. Did Hasan [the Egyptian soldier] reveal his secret? They approached the trench and sat on its edge with their legs dangling.
> "Tell me, what is your name?" Hasan turned to Henriko.
> "Muhammad," answered Henriko with a slight hesitation.
> "Listen, my dear boy," said Hasan seriously, "I risked my life for you. The minute my mates in the tent suspected you are a Jewish spy, I understood that this is true, and for a few moments I fought with myself. Should I betray you or not? Finally, the person of Hasan, the good peasant overcame the person of Hasan the slave, Hasan the mercenary soldier who is subservient to his master and kisses the tip of his whip. We have common enemies my boy. The enemy is illiteracy, disease, people who do not toil and who benefit from the labour of others. These wars themselves which are completely unnecessary as well as the hatred between man and man and people against people. Did I have to desert my land and my fields in order to come here and fight you? This is an injustice that tears the sky asunder to shed blood in your fields which are transformed through your labour and efforts from a desert to a garden of God . . .
> "You [the Israelis] must defeat the Naftuzis [Naftuzi was the name of the Egyptian officer in charge of Hasan]. You must win. One day will come when we shall also be able to defeat them on the banks of the Nile, but first you must defeat them properly and remove their stupid pride . . ."
> "And what should we do next?"
> "First of all, take this," Hasan handed Henriko a piece of paper.
> "A piece of paper?" asked Henriko with surprise.
> "This is a sketch of the cannon positions under the command of Abdullah Naftuzi. These cannons destroy your homes. These cannons kill your good people. These cannons must be destroyed and smashed."(Mosinson 1975: 94-5)

The positive Arab is represented as a woman, Aziza, who falls in love with one of the Jewish prisoners in Yigal Mosinson's *Hasambah in the Cave of Turkelin*. Her father sends her brother Mahmud to kill her for her treason, but the brother is also converted to the right way and turns against his father:

"You are a devil, not a father," grumbled Mahmud. "What damage did Aziza cause you? What damage did I cause you? Why are we destined to die if not merely because of your stupidity and ignorance. You live like people lived many thousands of years ago, like a primitive and not like human beings in the twentieth century ought to live." (Mosinson 1973: 155)

Abner Karmeli takes this logic to a more radical conclusion in his book, *The Young Sportsmen Return*. The evolution of the consciousness of a group of Arab football players from Nablus who decide to join the destiny of Israel and defend the dignity of Israel in the world of sport, is outlined as follows:

Some of the Arabic-speaking youths began to believe that they are the descendants of the ancient Israelites who remained in the country and did not depart to the Diaspora after the destruction of the country by the Romans. Following the occupation of the country by the Arabs the majority of the Israelite residents of the country were compelled against their will to subscribe to the religion of the conquerors and their customs. Now, so these Arab youths believe, the time has come to return to the bosom of their true people, the people of Israel, and participate in its great and glorious revival in its country as equal partners. (Karmeli n.d.: 25)

Thus the development is pretty clear. The youths in question change from Arabs to Arabic speakers, then to the descendants of the ancient Israelites, and finally to complete assimilation. Though clearly portrayed in positive terms, this kind of positive Arab is ineffective because he completely ceases to be an Arab. This is perhaps why he does not appear frequently in the literature.

Finally, very rarely did I find in the literature reviewed Arab characters that are portrayed as positive in and of themselves, irrespective of ideological considerations or political situations. One such rare portrayal is presented in Eliezer Semoli's *The People of the Beginning*. Tiqvah, the wife of the hero, is pregnant and in labour. Her husband Hermoni rushes her to the railway station to get her to the hospital in the neighbouring city. She begins labour in the train on the way to the hospital:

The passengers of the carriage panicked. The young men came to the compartment frightened, and carefully put their heads through the door of the compartment where the pregnant woman was lying. Their faces became serious and they sighed quietly.

"She is about to deliver," said Hermoni in desperation. "Friends, is there no woman in the carriage?"

"No, there is no woman in the carriage," announced one of the young men with a sigh . . .

Suddenly the old Bedouin emerged out of his corner and approached the compartment where Tiqvah lay.

"What is the matter, my brother?" he asked, adjusting the *hatta* and and the *'aqal* on his head and rubbing his black eyes.

"A woman is about to deliver," answered one of the peasant passengers whispering a prayer.

"Where?" called the old man in surprise.

"Here, my brother."

"By God," called the old man with great compassion. "Get moving, people," he called and pushed the passengers aside, cutting through them. "Hurry, get out of here, all of you!"

With a swift movement he removed his *'abaya* and handed it over to Hermoni to shelter the compartment where the delivering woman lay. Hermoni froze in his place. He watched the old Bedouin with grateful eyes clumsily blocking his way to Tiqvah.

"Don't be afraid, my son," the old man calmed him with a good smile. "God is merciful."

The old man whispered a prayer and watched Hermoni who stood there confused and trembling with soft and compassionate eyes.

"Do not be afraid my daughter, do not be afraid," the old man calmed Tiqvah behind the screen. "If God wills, everything will end well, everything will end in peace."

All of a sudden the carriage was shot through with a sharp scream of a rebellious and protesting voice, the voice of a new man on earth. Hermoni was all confused. With one rapid movement he removed his white shirt, entered the compartment of the mother and covered with it the red creature who cried and whimpered incessantly.

"Give me your son," said the old man, relieved, and stretched his hands towards Hermoni. "That's it. Everything is over. Deliver your thanks to God."

"Hurray!" shouted the railway workers in the carriage of honour of the mid-wife, "Hurray! Hurray!" Hermoni covered Tiqvah with a blanket and his eyes poured tears. The mother lay down swooning and the old Bedouin attended to the new born like a good mother, like a good mid-wife. (Semoli 1953: 150-2)

As noted above, such references are rare. One can cite similar references in Binyamin Tamuz's *A Boat Sails into the Sea,* Karah Feder's *Let Us Make Peace,* and Deborah Omer's *The Border inside the Heart.* In this last title the author attempts to deal with the relationship between the two peoples. In this context we find the following rare description:

During the night, the city Beit Shean was conquered by our forces, and in the morning there passed along the yard of the Kibbutz the convoy of Arab refugees from the conquered city. They made their way towards the Jordan River. I saw mothers, carrying their children with parcels on their backs and in their eyes the terror of war. The heavy convoys moved slowly and in great sadness, they descended towards the Jordan and crossed over it to the other side to the Kingdom of Jordan. They fled from here, from the war, from the defeat. In this long convoy I also saw Abdallah . . . for a moment I wanted to shout after him: Abdallah wait! Why are you fleeing? Indeed we are neighbours and in fact we could be friends. Stay here. Nobody will do you any harm. Do not run away Abdallah. Do not leave this valley, this entrance to the garden of Eden. But I did not say anything. I did not turn to him. I saw him descend towards the Jordan. (Omer 1973: 21)

Although they were friends, the woman kept silent and said nothing. This Arab remained a positive character in the mind of the silent woman but her very silence is quite consistent with Zionist philosophy. Liberal Zionists do not endorse what happened to the Palestinian Arab people, yet because of their commitment to Zionism they remain silent. They also lie. We know that the Palestinian Arab population of Beit Shean were consciously, deceitfully and forcibly expelled from the city (see above pp. 34-5) and yet the woman in the narrative quoted above refers to the exodus as flight rather than deliberate expulsion.

7. The Palestinian Arab Fighter and the Arab Soldier

Palestinian Fighters

Gangs and Robbers

"The Arab gangs plotted then to destroy all that was built by generations of pioneers" (Danni 1958: 95). Such is the description in the literature of the resistance of the Palestinian Arabs: gangs who wish to destroy "all that was built by generations of pioneers". Of course there is no attempt to explain to the child readers what the Arabs' reasons are for fighting. This structural omission has been discussed in detail in Chapter 5.

How then is the Palestinian Arab resistance depicted? Consider the following illustration:

> When the blood riots in the Land of Israel erupted, Sheikh Abdallah Abu Sitta took the leadership of the gangs of rioters and began organizing the attacks on the Hebrew lines of transport; shooting at the settlements, murder by ambush, mining of roads, all these were planned and administered by him. He travelled in a white jeep which he "nicked" from the British Army Camp at Nuseirat. He incited and directed the Bedouins to war against the Jews. (Meitiv 1972: 73)

The stories are transmitted from one person to another:

> I once heard, four or five days ago, how Rasin the guard told my father that the Arabs are organizing gangs in order to attack Jewish settlements. My father told him: "No matter; we will prepare for them a warm welcome." (Ofek 1969b: 90)

And thus the children can draw their own conclusions:

> "I now understand why Ahmad told us not to turn about here on our own . . . He did not want the gangs to discover us.
> "And also the Arab horseman whom we saw yesterday galloping on his horse is surely one of the gang, probably its communication man," said Michah. (Ofek 1969b: 91)

All the children's literature relating to the events before and during the

1948 war, irrespective of the date of publication, refer to the resistance of the Palestinian Arabs as gang resistance. The Arab member of the "gang" is depicted as devoid of conscience and cruel. In one such story, for example, a number of Jewish children are taken captive by members of "Arab gangs" and are taken for interrogation to the head of the "gang". Before they enter the tent of the head of the "gang", they are instructed by their guards as follows:

> "Do you see that large tent over there? That is the tent of the Commander." (He pronounced the word "Commander" with a special "o".) "You must tell him only the truth. He does not like lies. He recognizes immediately who tells the truth and who lies. He has such eyes that nothing escapes them. Do you understand? You must tell him everything, on the Haganah and the weapons and where the weapons are hidden. If you tell the truth you will get from him many gifts . . . whereas if you lie: do you see there on top of a hill a post with a rope dangling from it? This is the gallows. The noose is placed around the neck — and that's it, do you understand? That's that . . ." (Dominitz 1956: 43)

In another story, the author presents the Arabs in the most cruel manner, at least in so far as the imagination of young children is concerned. The following quote illustrates the depiction of the character of the Arab fighter in the most despicable manner: "There will be enough women for every one of us. Inshallah there will be enough. The boys who excel in the fighting will also get an extra woman. Hurray! We will show them, these Jew dogs" (Lieberman 1953: 85). That is, not only will every fighter get a woman, but the outstanding fighter will get an extra woman. In other words, the Arab fighter does not fight for principle, he fights for gain. The presentation of the Arab fighter as a cruel gangster is strengthened and underlined through the utilization of a common procedure in this literature, namely the presentation of the Arab case through an Arab character. Thus in Yehudah Salu's *Fire in the Mountains*, the Jewish boy thanks the Arab who helped him and saved him from the murderers. The following dialogue takes place:

> "Ali," I said to my new friend, "I know that you saved my life."
> "Don't talk about it, O Child," said Ali. "Indeed I could not hand you over to these people. They do not take prisoners, and they do not treat the wounded. They are bloodthirsty animals."
> "And you are not one of them?" I asked.
> "No," said Ali. "I stayed here to guard the school and the school property. But this is very difficult. They destroy everything."
> "Where did you learn to speak Hebrew?" I asked him. Ali finished dressing his legs and sat in the chair. "It all happened by coincidence," he said. "If it were not for sheer chance I would be like them all . . ."
> "That's it," said Ali . . . "I failed in everything. The school is transformed into a den of robbers. The children which I raised, my former pupils, joined the gang. Three are already killed. They were your age. The smaller ones are in Hebron — also from them I shall see no fruit. All that I did was like a drop in

the ocean and also that was useless. One swallow does not a summer make . . ." (Salu 1970: 41)

Through this procedure, the "good Arab" confirms the Zionist stereotype as superimposed over the reality of his fighting people; namely that they are cruel gangsters. He abhors the fact that his people are fighting and that there is no good Arab other than himself — "the single swallow". He makes this statement before a fighting Jewish child who, had he succeeded in getting to his destination, would have surely killed Arabs and "liberated Jerusalem". Thus the Jew is depicted as fighting for principles whereas the Arabs are depicted as lacking principles: a collection of gangsters, robbers and murderers.

In parallel with the development of the image of the Arab as a thief (see above pp. 72-4), the literature introduces the image of the Arab robber who, unlike the thief, attacks the Jew to rob and kill, taking possession of his goods by force and not by stealthy treachery. In other words, the robber is a fighter who carries out his action by force of arms.

One of the few books in the literature that meets good literary and artistic standards is *The People of the Beginning* by Eliezer Semoli. It is one of the classic works in the field and I regard it as very important. In this book, as in the rest of the literature, there is a distinction between the Arab as a thief and the Arab as a robber. The following quote will clearly indicate how the Palestinian fighters are reduced to robbers whose aim is to destroy and steal. Nevertheless, the author could not completely ignore the fact that this was a war against foreign occupation — namely the Zionist occupation of the land of Palestine.

> Hermoni came to him and put his hand on his head and told him with trembling voice: "Do not cry, Eitan, do not despair. Your name is Eitan ['firm' in Hebrew] and you must stand firm . . . We have become used to the attacks of robbers and more than once myself and your mother were balanced on the borderline between life and death and came out of the trial whole. It is already for a quarter of a century that we have stood guard in the process of building the country. We never recoiled. The robbers can set fire to the barn but not to the aspirations of the suffering people. We clung with our fingernails to the rocks of this country and no force in the world can move us away." (Semoli 1953: 265)

It is clear that the people referred to here as robbers are Palestinian fighters, fighting to liberate their country. They sustained a war against Jewish settlement, purchase of lands by the Zionist movement, and the dispossession of the Palestinian Arab population. Consider the following description:

> Barely did we begin to leave the ruins when a shower of bullets descended upon us from the direction of the river. The sound of galloping horses and the cries of robbers eager to fight could be heard over the ancient stone bridge...
> Do not be afraid. I will carry the ploughshare to Tel Hai. Under no

circumstances will it fall into the hands of the murderers.

The robbers continued shooting. The bullets whistled above our heads and zoomed about us like flies of death. We ran across the plain, hunched in a loose line, running and taking turns — three shooting backwards and three advancing towards Tel Hai. (Semoli 1972: 110)

The battles sustained by the Palestinian Arab resistance in 1920 against Tel Hai and Kefar Giladi are well-known chapters in its history. Here, as in all other Israeli Hebrew children's books, the patriotic fighters are reduced to robbers, although the literature does occasionally betray inconsistencies. For instance, in one story, the children are perplexed at the Arab "gangsters" whom they meet:

"This young man in the *kuffiyya* [the Arab headdress], he spoke good Hebrew," said Menachem. "I had the feeling when he spoke that he was Jewish."

"I also had such a feeling," said Zvi. "I wonder how he can be a member of a gang if he knows Hebrew so well." (Dominitz 1956: 52)

The subject of the Arab robbers has become a central theme for many Israeli Hebrew adventure books. It has been developed as an independent theme, not directly related to the war situation in the country. Yigal Mosinson is a prolific writer of cheap, venomous, anti-Arab children's books. One of his books in the "Hasambah" series is entitled *Hasambah and the Horse Robbers*. The three robbers are Said, Mustafa and Ibrahim. The story revolves around the Jewish youth gang of Hasambah who go out to fight these robbers and, of course, win in the end. Note the following typical description:

Mustafa Jamali realized that he was trapped. He rose lazily from his seat and contemplated in his heart that these Jewish children are really some fellows; real heroes. Indeed, they dared to arrest him, Mustafa Jamali, the famous robber with the scar across his cheek. (Mosinson 1951: 104)

But one must emphasize that the Arab robber is generally connected in image to the Palestinian fighter, who is invariably presented as primitive and uncivilized. Note the following illustration: Tommy is a Jewish youth who arrives in a pioneer immigration ship. Following disembarkation, he heads for a Jewish village, but before arriving at his destination, he hears shooting. He is not certain that the place in the distance where he is heading is indeed a Jewish village. He deliberates the question as follows:

Who is really the enemy? Who are the attackers and who are the attacked? He tended to assume that the attackers were Arab gangs since, as he had heard, the Arabs do not have in their villages modern lighting; also the spacious shape of the buildings testified that the inhabitants were Jews. (Yefet n.d.: 38)

The Incited Mob
When the Palestinian Arab people rose to resist by force the occupation of their country and the plans to dispossess them of their lands, the rebellion and

resistance are depicted in the Israeli Hebrew literature as the rioting of a mob incited by its leaders.

> Among the Arabs there were people who incited the population telling them that the Jews will take away their country. The masses of incited Arabs only waited for convenient opportunities to shed Jewish blood like water and also rob the Jews of their property. But the hatred of the Arabs for the Hebrew community also increased more and more. Their leaders did not cease from inciting them to believe that the desire of the Jews is to take their lands out of their hands, and they instigated them against the Hebrew community and sent them to attack the new settlement, rob their farms and murder their residents. (Danni 1958:92)

Indeed, today one can clearly state that the warning of the Arab leaders regarding the Zionist dispossession of the Palestinian Arab people and the appropriation of their country and land was correct. It is also important to note that the Hebrew authors of this literature could not conceive of the Arab public as intelligent or autonomous. The people do not fight because they are motivated by principle or by a clear, rational objective but merely because they have been irrationally incited. Consider the following:

> In early May 1921, irresponsible Arabs, devoid of conscience, incited a wild Arab mob in Jaffa, telling them lies about the Jews of Tel-Aviv and moving them to descend upon their Jewish neighbours and massacre them.
> Hundreds of porters, sailers, hot-headed hooligans, mercenary profiteers, and blood-thirsty rioters took knives and iron bars in their hands, and on one peaceful innocent spring morning attacked the border quarters of Jaffa–Tel Aviv, which were inhabited by Jews and Arabs who had been living together in good neighbourliness for many dozens of years. They massacred old people, women and innocent children. Like cruel animals of prey they charged into the homes of the new [Jewish] immigrants of the border of Jaffa–Tel Aviv: little isolated houses, packed with pioneer men and women who only yesterday ascended to the land of Israel from Poland and Lithuania. They were victims of a cruel massacre. The residents of Tel Aviv had not yet understood the design of the incited rioting mob and tens of new immigrants and veteran residents of border quarters were butchered with knives and beheaded with iron bars . . .
> For three days the blood-thirsty mob rioted, injured, set property on fire, robbed and destroyed, and the Arab British Police watched and did not raise a finger. On the contrary; every Jew who dared to take any weapon of defence into his hands and go out against the rioters was placed under arrest by the Arab British 'guardians of the Law' and thrown into jail. (Semoli 1972:127)

The concept of incitement is also introduced in descriptions of organized Arab attacks. Thus the author undermines the credibility of the attack: the Arabs do not really wish to take part in the attack – they are incited.

> The Arabs emerged from among the hills which surround the Kibbutz in the North and North West. They descended on the Kibbutz with savage screams and without any plan or order. These were not soldiers, rather these were incited villagers who, waving their weapons, descended down the slope. Their

attack strategy was based on their numerical superiority. They numbered a few hundred . . . (Gal 1958:96)

The author intimates that these could not be soldiers or guerrilla commandos or any other kind of fighters, because they have been incited. They have no object in the war because they are mindless and have been pushed into fighting by their leaders. All the authors, almost without exception, emphasize that without such incitement, war would not have broken out; peace would have prevailed in the region. Needless to say, according to this literature only the Arab leadership incited its people to fight. The general import of the literature is that the Palestinian Arabs fought solely because they were incited. There was no question of ideology or self-defence.

It is interesting to juxtapose this description, which is bound to make a deep impression on the young reader and inculcate hatred in the Jewish youth for Arabs, with another description which concentrates on the relationships between the Arabs of Jaffa and the Jews of Tel Aviv, but from a different point of view; namely that of Jewish heroism as expressed in the attack by the Haganah forces on the city of Jaffa:

> The city of Jaffa, neighbouring Tel Aviv, is today a Hebrew city and the Jews who are residents of the city walk in its streets proud and free. It was, however, different before the establishment of the State. Jaffa was then an Arab city and the majority of its residents were Arabs among whom there were people who did not view favourably the residents of neighbouring Tel Aviv and planned evil designs against their neighbours whom they considered to be bad people.
>
> Arab sharp-shooters used to take positions in houses bordering with Tel Aviv in the quarters of Manshiyya, Hasan Bek, and Abu Kabir. They would snipe during day and night, endanger the border residents and the pedestrians in the Hebrew city . . .
>
> Members of the Haganah refused to accept the fact of the enemy blocking routes and roads . . . This situation continued for a long time until it became unbearable, companies of Jewish Sappers would penetrate occasionally into the Arab quarters to place explosives and sabotage enemy positions and concentrations of Arab gangs. But the enemy persevered . . . Then one day the Commanders convened in the Headquarters of the Haganah in the Southern front of Tel Aviv to develop military plans. They came to the conclusion that they had only one way open to them – that was to expel them completely, uproot the enemy from all its positions and houses and clear the way. (Weinberg 1956:127-9)

This narrative is quite explicit and outlines the pattern of Jewish attacks on the Arab community of Jaffa as well as the orchestration of the expulsion of the Palestinian Arab residents of Jaffa. Yet when the Arabs organized their defence against these attacks, they are depicted as a "mob devoid of conscience".

Infiltrators

After the establishment of the state of Israel in 1948, the Palestinian Arab population wanted to re-enter their country even if "illegally". Some wished to return and attempt to stay. Others wished to return in order to take out valuables such as money, jewellery and gold, which they had left behind at the time of their expulsion, in order to build a new life in their countries of dispersion. Still others wished to join members of their family who remained under Israeli occupation. It was only a small minority who wished to enter illegally in order to continue the war against Israel. These people carried no political or military weight. There is no doubt that some wished to use the opportunity to steal Jewish property and sell it to make a living, but this again was a marginal and quite insignificant phenomenon.

But the Israeli authorities depicted the Palestinian "infiltrators" as enemies of the state whose only aim was to kill innocent residents: old people, women and children. In addition, Israeli policy was dictated by strong ideological considerations in that the return of the Palestinian Arab people to their country would be an inconceivable disaster. The state of Israel has persistently refused to recognize that the Palestinian Arab people have any right to return to their homeland; this refusal still applies today. The Palestinian Arab "infiltrator" figured centrally in the Israeli policy of retaliation operations, namely Israeli-initiated attacks across the newly established borders into the territory of the Arab states and particularly the Palestinian Arab refugee camps in the Gaza Strip. For the Israeli Hebrew children's literature of the first decade following the establishment of the state of Israel, the subject of the "infiltrators" is central. Why do the Palestinians infiltrate into the country? According to the majority of the authors, they infiltrate in order to steal and kill.

> The previous night was a night of horror; a night that shocked even the residents of Ramat Ha-Makhtesh, who were used to the manoeuvres of the infiltrators . . . There was not a single week without the penetration of the infiltrators into the farm: robbing, destroying and escaping. But this time the attack was most daring. They penetrated to the centre of the village and even broke into the physicians' room and stole expensive medical equipment and medicines. (Eliav 1955:8)

The subject of "infiltration" is the only subject in the literature reviewed which has an element of reciprocity in that there are also stories describing Jews who "infiltrate" Arab states. Needless to say, this infiltration is completely justified by the authors. There are many Hebrew childrens' books which describe "infiltration" by a group of children, or even by individual children – Israeli Jews – into Arab states to fight the Arabs. This Jewish "infiltration" is pursued for motives very similar to those of the Palestinian Arab "infiltrators" into Israel. For instance, we have one such book by Haim Eliav entitled *The Children of the Old City and the Treasure of Baghdad*. It tells the story of a Jewish child who immigrated with his family to Palestine and who knows that his father had treasure of gold and silver in his house in Baghdad before his departure. With a number of friends he infiltrates into Iraq after travelling across Jordan, and through a sequence of successful adventures arrives in Baghdad at his father's house, locates the treasure and then returns with friends and other Jews to the state of Israel.

This infiltration from Israel into the Arab states is of course judged as reasonable. The reader is clearly encouraged to consider infiltration to Baghdad to retrieve the family treasure as highly positive, whereas if a Palestinian Arab infiltrates for exactly the same purpose into the state of Israel, the reader learns that Jewish settlements are thereby endangered.

Jewish infiltration is viewed by the literature under review from a humanitarian point of view. It seems that the authors have no particular difficulty in justifying anything, even killing or sabotage, that is done by a Jewish infiltrator into an Arab country in the course of the struggle for his life or his state. This does not apply to the Palestinian Arab infiltrator.

The Saboteurs

After the July 1952 revolution in Egypt and the rise of its President Gamal Abdul Nasser to leadership of the Arab world, Israel initiated a policy of military attacks against Egypt. The most notorious attacks were carried out by Unit 101 led by Ariel Sharon, later Minister of Agriculture and subsequently Minister of Defence in the Begin government. Unit 101 was formed as a special force designated to pursue terrorists and carry out retaliatory operations beyond the borders. The story of its operations is now published by Uri Milstein (*Unit 101,* 1968).

The Unit operated mainly in the West Bank and Gaza Strip. In Gaza, it penetrated into refugee camps and engaged in the straight murder of citizens. The objectives of these attacks and other operations inside Egypt, as we now know from official statements and publications, were to humiliate President Gamal Abdul Nasser, distance him from the West, and motivate the West to launch a war against Egypt. The policy proved successful and resulted in the 1956 tripartite attack by Britain, France and Israel on the United Arab Republic.

As a result of these attacks, the Palestinian Arab population began to organize guerrilla groups known at the time as *fedayin* (correctly transliterated as *fidaiyyun* meaning "those who sacrifice themselves"). The *fedayin* concentrated on penetrations into Israel and carried out largely ineffectual operations. It was the existence of the *fedayin* and the persistence of *fedayin* penetrations that fed Israeli propaganda and was presented by Israel as the official reason for its participation in the Sinai campaign, jointly with Britain and France, in 1956.

Fedayin activity was effectively discontinued after the 1956 war for various reasons, largely relating to internal Egyptian and Jordanian policies and the state of inter-Arab relations. Given the structure of the *fedayin* organization, it could not sustain its operations without the active military support of the host state. This reflected the political assumption that the Palestinian problem would be solved not by the Palestinian Arab people themselves but rather by Arab leaders. When these leaders failed to solve the problem, a new initiative of Palestinian organization was begun, led by young Palestinian Arabs who decided to bring the destiny of Palestine back to the Palestinian people and force the leaders of the Arab states and the world to act to solve their problem. The Palestine Liberation Organization (PLO) was established in 1964 and has been recognized since 1974 as the sole legitimate representative of the Palestinian people.

The military operations of the various Palestinian organizations persisted without interruption from 1965. The operations were carried out by the various Palestinian organizations representing different ideologies and political analyses, but from the point of view of the Israeli authorities, all Palestinian organizations were reduced to terrorist organizations, and every Palestinian person who joined them was reduced to a saboteur.

Following the 1967 war and the spectacular Israeli victory and occupation of the Golan Heights, West Bank, Gaza Strip and Sinai Peninsula, the literature reflects the new political situation as it consolidated under the Israeli occupation. Consider the following discussion:

At that moment there was a knock at the door and a young man entered the room. His hair was black and kinky. His face betrayed open anger and his eyes glowed with suppressed hatred. Mahmud's wife left the room. The young man collapsed into one of the chairs and smashed his clenched fist onto the table until the plates and the cups danced all over the surface. "No matter," he muttered angrily, "a day will come when the Jews will pay dearly for all they have done to us. They believe that they have won the war, but they are mistaken. Without the Americans who came to their aid . . ." Mahmud cut the angry young man short.

"You too, Said? [Said is the 'saboteur' in the story.] Drop this silly talk. You hear some lie on the Cairo radio and you immediately believe it and pass it on. We ourselves are to blame for our own defeat and we did not listen to the voice of reason. The Jews repeatedly offered us peace and we blocked our ears and did not hear. All the time we are merely gnashing our teeth, talk of revenge and educate our children to blind hatred, then here are the results . . ."

Said's lips curled with a derisory smile. "And you believe that the Jews really wanted peace? They planned all the time to attack us and conquer our Holy countries . . ."

Mahmud shook his head in desperation. "Said, you are a hopeless idiot. The Jews number merely two million people in their country and we, the Arabs, have twenty states and one hundred million people . . . do you really believe that they planned to conquer all the Arab countries?"

"Yes, of course I believe it. Even Cairo radio announced that the Jews began the war in order to dominate the Arab nation."

Mahmud jumped up and started pacing up and down the room. "Cairo radio," he said in open anger, "you still are not aware of the lie industry of

Cairo radio? Did you forget, Said? Just a few weeks ago, the announcers of Cairo radio claimed a brilliant victory and told us that our forces entered Tel Aviv, conquered Tiberias, destroyed Safed and marched on Haifa . . . Instead, the Jews are sitting in Hebron and Jericho, along the Suez Canal, and on the Golan Heights. And you still believe the fables of one thousand and one nights of Cairo radio?"

Said waved his hand in contempt. "It doesn't matter what happened in the past. We shall never reconcile ourselves to Jewish rule over us – there will be no peace between the Arab countries and the Jews, never. I see that you are lost, Mahmud. I come to you as a neighbour in order to warn you that we will not tolerate collaborators with the Jews." Said shot a cunning look at his neighbour. "They say that yesterday two Jews came to you and sat in your home for over an hour. There are eyes everywhere, Mahmud . . ." (Vardi 1971:57–60)

Said represents here the Palestinian resistance. He is active in a "saboteur" network in Jerusalem. He is presented as being unwilling to understand what is going on. He makes no distinction between Jew and Israeli and foolishly accepts all that is announced over Cairo Radio. He appears "stupid" because he is unwilling to reconcile himself to the occupation. The young reader is told that the Palestinians wish to fight the Jews because the Jews aim to conquer all the Arab countries. The real motive for the Palestinian resistance, namely the occupation, is ignored. For the author, the fact that Said lives under occupation is not a sufficient reason for resistance. Needless to say, the story ends with the capture of all members of the sabotage network.

In another story by Abner Karmeli, *The Young Sportsmen Return*, the author presents the Palestinian fighters as inferior and very cruel, the antithesis of the Israelis. The story develops around two members of the Israeli national sports team who have been kidnapped together with the deputy trainer of the team. It is interesting that the author introduces into the story Jewish traitors who collaborate with the "saboteurs", a very rare element in Israeli Hebrew children's literature. Another party in the plot and an ally of the "gang of murderers" is the Soviet Union. The young reader is encouraged to understand that the Communist Jews are traitors and collaborators with the enemies of the state:

"Everything will soon be made clear to you," said Rafi. "I ought to clarify the situation to you briefly because they will soon come to deal with you and we shall not be able to talk freely anymore. Well . . . a special saboteur organization was set up whose objective is to undermine and befoul the decent social relations that are forming between the Arab and Hebrew residents in the Land of Israel. They do not want these residents to live in peace in one country and they want to bring about partition of the homeland and its cleavage into two separate countries as a first step to our final annihilation. The thing that annoys the saboteur organizations and our Arab enemies, as well as their Russian patrons and allies, is the close and beautiful cooperation that has been established between the Arabs and the Hebrews in the Land of Israel, especially in the field of sports, the summit of which is the participation of Arab and Hebrew players in complete fraternity in the national football team in the Land of Israel. Our team will leave for the World Cup competition in Spain and thus demonstrate this fraternity before the eyes of the whole world . . .

"Well, in order to prevent this, the Arab States and the Soviet Union have set up a special Arab saboteur organization with the aim of liquidating our team. This saboteur organization was connected with a number of traitors in the Hebrew community in this country. Traitors of the worst kind who work in the service of the enemy; young men who lack in their heart any feeling for the homeland and the people, who desire to betray the whole of the Land of Israel to complete Arab rule, which will prevent the return of the remainder of the people of Israel from the Diaspora to their homeland and liquidate all the Israelis that were born in this country or who have already immigrated here."

"How did you come to know these things, Rafi?" asked Alon . . .

"I will soon tell you how these were revealed . . . I say this with despair, but it is pointless to ignore the truth, and this is the truth: traitors, servants of the enemy . . . [who] hate anyone who loves the Land of Israel as a homeland, which they cannot understand. Such traitors have given their hand in assistance to the Arab saboteurs in order to destroy the national team of Israel."

Rafi continued with his lips pressed tight. "Two of these traitors masqueraded as armed Israeli soldiers and asked for a ride with the national trainer, Abraham ha-Gelili, who passed by in his car some five weeks ago. They kidnapped him and brought him to the headquarters of the saboteurs at a small hotel in Nablus which is under the complete control of the saboteurs. Here, their hypnotist succeeded in hypnotizing him and thus brought him to a state whereby he will carry out all their instructions without protest. They have a hypnotist who is a master in the art." (Karmeli n.d.: 76–8)

This is a fairly sophisticated line of argument. It of course ignores the reality of Israeli colonization, the establishment of Israeli Jewish settlements throughout the post-1967 occupied territories, the policy of mass deportation, collective punishments, the spraying of crops with defoliant poison and the repeated, sustained demonstrations by the Palestinian Arab population against Israeli occupation and policies of repression.

Reality is ignored in order to equip the young reader with false notions to the effect that the Palestinian Arabs living under Israeli occupation are happy with their situation, resigned to the denial of their independence, and that they have good relations with the Jews. On the other hand, the PLO, the Arab states, the Soviet Union and Israeli Jewish Communists refuse to accept the establishment of this peaceful situation, and are therefore engaged in evil plots to destroy it.

It is important to point out that there is a consistent inability in the literature reviewed to relate to the development of Palestinian society and Palestinian resistance, or to changes in the ideology of the resistance.

The essential features of the Palestinian fighters as portrayed in the literature remain unaltered. They are presented as lowly, ugly, dangerous, thieving and cowardly. No change is indicated in the level of Palestinian organization or its method of fighting. The Palestinian resistance is conceptualized throughout as consisting of gangs of robbers aiming to rob and kill the Jews; only the terms of reference change. The term "robbers" before 1948 was replaced with the term "*fedayin*" between 1948 and 1967, and then with the term "saboteurs" following the 1967 war. The Palestinian resistance is presented as devoid of any political content and reduced to blind revenge and criminality. The literature implies that the Palestinian resistance must be distorted and reduced in order to present the Zionist case convincingly. This may be an indication of how shaky that case is.

The Israeli "Superman"

Throughout the literature the Israeli soldier is portrayed as a "superman", not only in the spectacular nature of his attacks but also in the quality of his determination:

> "In order that none of us remain alive to be interrogated by torture by the enemy, should the aircraft be shot down before we reach our target," said Meno with a fascinating smile, "we will not take with us any parachutes. We will all be smashed with the crashing plane and the Egyptians will never know what we aimed to do in the Sinai."
>
> "We cannot make this demand on you and your people, to be crashed voluntarily together with your aircraft in the event that it be shot down," cried out General Gevariyahu.
>
> "You do not make this demand", explained Meno. "We demand this from ourselves, on the clear understanding that there is no other alternative. And now gentlemen, do you endorse the operation?"
>
> Those present, all of them veteran and experienced commanders, fixed their astonished eyes on him and then exchanged questioning looks among themselves. "We endorse," said at last General Amiti, the representative of the Navy . . . "Me too," said General Saar, the representative of the Air force . . . (Karmeli 1973:68)

Entire series of books have been published in which the hero is the Israeli "superman". The "Hasambah" series by Yigal Mosinson, portraying the adventures of a group of Israeli youth who risk their lives to save the homeland and fight the Arab enemy, consisted of over 20 volumes.

The "Dannidin" books by Sarig narrate the adventures of another Israeli "superman" hero, an invisible child who succeeds in penetrating into the Arab states undetected to obtain secrets and assist Israeli soldiers:

> At that time Dannidin's father, Mr Din, returned home from his work, sat on the balcony and read the evening paper. His face was grave as he read in the paper the reports of the threats of the Arabs to destroy Israel and of the large armies that they concentrated at our borders.
>
> "We must do something on this matter," he said to his wife. "It is not

possible to sit at rest when the enemy is planning to attack us from all sides."

"And we do not even know where the main attack will be launched," said his wife Mrs Din.

"Do you know," Mr Din told her with a smile, "had our Danni turned invisible again he could have penetrated any Arab command and brought with him the maps indicating exactly the plans of the enemy."

"Indeed," said Mrs Din, "it is a pity that he cannot again turn invisible for a while. He would have brought great benefit to Israel had he spied against the Arabs." (Sarig 1968a: 40–1)

Needless to say, Dannidin succeeds in penetrating the enemy defences and discovering all the secrets of the war, thus securing Israel's victory.

The series of "Azit" by Motah Gur, the former Israeli Chief of Staff, portrays the Israeli "superman" in the person of a female dog. The series consists of three volumes, *Azit in the Palaces of Cairo* (1971), *Azit in the Desert of Judea* (no date) and *Azit the Paratroop Bitch* (1963). In these books the former Israeli Chief of Staff develops a plot in which an Israeli female dog proves capable of defeating the Arab world. Azit the female dog succeeds in reaching Gamal Abdul Nasser. She is present at his most important meetings and can thus transmit to Israel all the secrets of Egypt:

> More than anything else Fuad feared the Israelis. His fear of unexpected action by the Israelis sometimes drove him mad. In every piece of furniture or behind any object the terrible Israeli could be hidden or act by way of magic and witchcraft. How else could they have won all the wars? The physical proximity of Fuad to the leaders enabled the recorder hidden in Azit's collar to record every word very clearly . . . Fuad sat in the chair adjacent to the wall next to Nasser. From his chair he could view the entire room, especially the entrances. Azit stretched herself calmly between Fuad's chair and the comfortable sofa on which Nasser and his guest sat. Nasser stretched his hand from time to time absent-mindedly and stroked her head. Azit raised her eyelids but did not shift her position and did not move her head. The visitor noticed Nasser's stroking, and hastened to ask him politely who was the beautiful dog, what was her name, her pedigree, her achievements. (Gur 1971: 134, 135)

The denigration of the Arab soldier is correlative to the elevation of the Israeli "superman". The Arab soldier is a coward; the Israeli "superman" is fearless. The Arab soldier is stupid; the Israeli "superman" is clever, etc. The narrative is always structured to demonstrate the Israeli "superman's" victory, not only in war, but in any competition with the Arab. Thus in Abner Karmeli's *The Young Sportsmen: Israel against Egypt,* the author describes a football match between an Israeli and an Egyptian team. The Egyptians succeed in delaying the two "supermen" of the Israeli team, and thus maintain a lead of 13 goals for most of the game. But when the two Israeli "supermen" land their plane right in the middle of the football pitch and join their team, they tip the balance 14–13 and secure victory over Egypt (Karmel 1963: 92–8).

What circumstances led to the creation of the Israeli "supermen"? The universal explanation throughout the literature is that the Jews have no alternative. They must be powerful because they have nowhere else to go. If they lose once they lose everything and for ever. The Jew is transformed into a "superman" because the Arabs wish to murder him for no reason other than that he is a Jew.

At the agricultural school there studied a number of Arab pupils. And then one bright day they left school because they had frequently heard recently that all the Jews would be slaughtered soon and then everything would fall into their hands and the school would be theirs. Why should they remain as pupils if tomorrow they could return as masters?

And indeed sometime later Moshkeh met one of these Arab pupils marching at the head of an incited Arab mob in Jaffa shouting: "Slaughter the Jews."

It was then that Moshkeh was as if made grown up again. Now he understood and comprehended why he had dreamed all these years about soldiers . . . His great hour has now arrived. Hebrew soldiers are now needed to defend the *yishuv*. He was certain that his mother and his father would understand him now and would tell him: "Moshkeh you were right. The *yishuv* needs soldiers. We thought that it would be possible to depend on these Arabs. But you were right and we were wrong." (Sadeh 1971: 39–40)

How does the Israeli "superman" behave at the hour of trial? His most prominent feature is his arrogance. A characteristic illustration is Abner Karmeli's story of the Special Reconnaissance Unit commissioned to penetrate into Egypt in a helicopter and hijack an Egyptian MiG 21 so that the Israeli army can examine the plane and develop an efficient defence against it. In the story the Special Reconnaissance Unit undertakes the assignment but their helicopter is intercepted by the Egyptians who launch eight MiG 21 aircraft to bring it down.

The eight MiG 21 aircraft took off one by one within one minute, with their jet engines roaring at a blood-freezing pitch from the huge airstrip of Naj Suleiman. In parallel the entire sophisticated, diversified and extensive defence system of their air base, and the accesses to the air base, was put into operational alert. Thousands of soldiers went into their positions around the air field, arming their weapons and keeping a watch with their senses sharpened sevenfold. Hundreds of projectors were lit and their beams began to search the sky and the ground. Dozens of anti-aircraft guns positioned in all the key positions of the base, began aiming their barrels, under radar instructions, in the direction of the approaching target. The entire huge system constructed to defend the Naj Suleiman field was quickly put on alert . . .

The soldiers listened with ultimate attention to the last astonishing instructions of their commander: "It is clear that we have no chance of confronting the huge sophisticated defence system of the Naj Suleiman field. If we are not discovered by radar, we will be discovered by the projectors. If we are not shot down by the fire of the machine gun positions, we will be shot down by the fire of the cannons or the missiles. And if we escape these, we will surely be destroyed by the MiG's themselves . . ."

"Can we now at last switch off the lights in the helicopter, Meno?" asked officer David Hameiri. "The Egyptians will be able to shoot it down with their pistols if we continue flying in full lights. The darkness will perhaps offer us a little bit of cover to hide . . ."

"Who said we wish to hide?" Meno cut him short, to everyone's astonishment. "The lights will remain on."

"But we are entering into Egyptian air space," announced the pilot at that very moment with a strange hoarseness in his voice . . .

"I hope that they will shoot us down near the Pyramids of Pithom and Rameses," Nisan Ziv said all of a sudden smiling from ear to ear, despite the hammering of his turbulent heart. "I always wanted to see what was the quality of the construction work of our forefathers . . ."

"The anti-aircraft guns of the Egyptian coastal defence opened fire at us," reported the pilot. "We are exactly over the first line of their defences. Do you want me to fly low, Meno? I could better evade their shells if I hover close to surface level."

"On the contrary fly even higher," ordered Meno to everyone's astonishment. "I want all the Egyptians in the area to be able to see us." (Karmeli 1971: 119–21)

Of course the helicopter is not hit and the Reconnaissance Unit succeeds in hijacking a MiG 21 and bringing it to Israel. This is how the Israeli "superman" is expected to behave. He is certain that neither the MiGs, nor the Egyptian guns, nor the missiles with their Soviet advisers could shoot down the helicopter. This arrogance reflects the weakness of the Arab armies. This particular book was published in 1971, four years after the June 1967 war. It was possible then for the Israeli "supermen" to demonstrate complete contempt of all human and professional values of the Egyptian soldier. The Israeli "superman" was confident that nothing could stop his helicopter: let all the Egyptians know that Israelis are penetrating to hijack a MiG 21. There is nothing they can do about it.

The Arab Soldier

From a review of the literature at hand, it is clear that no essential change took place in the image of the Palestinian Arab fighter following the Israeli–Arab wars of 1948, 1956, 1967 and 1973. But the image of the Arab armies and the Arab soldier does alter slightly and implicitly after the 1973 war. I will outline the relevant changes and their context separately. It is in order to point out here, however, that these changes relate to the fact that the 1973 war did not result in undisputed Israeli victory and that in the initial stages of the war the Israeli defences of the southern front along the Suez Canal and along the northeastern front in the Golan Heights were overrun by the Egyptian and Syrian armies respectively.

The two fronts of the 1973 war are depicted differently in the literature under review. In the north the Syrian army overran Israeli defences as well as the Israeli Jewish settlements of the Golan Heights. However, in the course of the war the Israeli army succeeded in reoccupying this territory and re-establishing the evacuated Jewish settlements. The shock of enemy tanks, and specifically Syrian tanks, entering Jewish settlements in the Golan Heights made an impact on the literature. The image of the Jew had to be altered in order to accommodate references to Israeli casualties, dead and wounded, which had hitherto been almost absent from the literature.

In the southern front the Israeli army never succeeded in recapturing the Bar Lev defences along the east bank of the Suez Canal, yet it is interesting that despite the evident success of the Egyptian and Syrian soldiers in the 1973 war the negative image of the Arab soldier was not altered. The literature does not explain, nor does it attempt to explain, how it could be that the Egyptian Arab soldier portrayed over three decades as a despicable and cowardly caricature could stand up to the superior Israeli soldier, and not only defeat all his attempts to reconquer the lost territories along the Suez Canal, but also take Israeli soldiers and officers prisoner. The authors of the literature reviewed could not separate the image of the Arab soldier from the image of the Arab in general. And thus even in those battles where the Arab soldier is successful, his image remains largely negative, despicable, cowardly, lying and devoid of human and military values. Given the ideological supremacy of Zionist philosophy in Israel and given the fact that until 1973 Israel was evidently successful in its wars against the Arabs, it was not possible for the authors of this literature to portray a positive image of the Arab soldier or allow for the development of a modern Arab soldier of the 20th century, who could successfully employ electronic equipment, sophisticated aircraft or advanced tanks. The image of the Arab soldier remains backward, and the responsibility for all Middle East wars is ascribed invariably to the Arab desire to destroy the Jewish state. Since the destruction of the Jewish state is identified as the supreme catastrophe, a holocaust, it is rendered legitimate in the literature to do anything to prevent it.

The Arab soldier hates the Jews. His hatred is blind and irrational. He wants to butcher the Jews only because they are Jews. The authors do not offer any detailed ideological or political explanation. They portray the Arab soldier as an out-and-out idiot. In one of the stories the author tells of Egyptian soldiers who "stand on guard" but all they do is spend their time playing cards. After presenting the soldiers in most humiliating terms, as if all they do is shout and curse each other, he attributes to them the following narrative: "'Tomorrow we will slaughter all the Jews,' shouted one of the card players, bearing his teeth like a rabid dog" (Mosinson 1975: 76). In the same story the author develops the theme of an Israeli youth successfully penetrating this Egyptian position and easily manipulating the foolishness of an Egyptian soldier.

Other authors predicate their story on a different shade of hatred:

The Syrian soldier advanced towards me with his eyes full of hatred, but I did not move. He directed the barrel of his gun to my heart and I continued to fix him with a cold glare and did not run away. Then when he stopped at the distance of just one step from me I raised my left leg in a circular movement, directed a strong kick at his gun and sent my fist straight into his mouth. The soldier dropped to the ground like a log of wood. (Ron-Feder 1971:121)

This description of the Syrian soldier as full of hatred is not unique. Generally the Arab soldier in the literature reviewed is motivated to fight by hatred and evil aspirations. This is how an Arab prisoner of war is described: "The skin of his face was pock-marked and porous. His eyes small and evil, his moustache pointed on either side of his face. His neck was thick and short" (Biber 1974: 117–18). Such descriptions would give the young reader the feeling that whatever this Arab prisoner is subjected to during his imprisonment and interrogation is legitimate simply because "this evil man" deserves to suffer the worst.

Why does the Arab soldier hate? Not only because it is his nature but also because he was educated to hate and because his government hates Israel and the Jews. This line is dominant in most of the books reviewed. In some books Arab leaders are mentioned by name, especially President Gamal Abdul Nasser; but most frequently it is the Syrian regime that is mentioned in this context.

The Syrian regime is known for its extremism and hatred of Israel and the Jews. We have information on the persecution of Jews by the authorities especially when border clashes between the Syrian army and the Israeli army take place. (Biber 1974:78)

The statement that the Syrian regime hates Israel and the Jews is posited in the literature reviewed as justifying any and every action by the Israeli army against Syria. The hatred of the Syrian regime and its alleged persecution of the Jews are presented as the outstanding features of an irrational enemy. The Israeli party to the conflict is portrayed both overtly and by implication as completely innocent of any such criminal irrationality. The young reader would never suspect that the Israeli regime is guilty of radical and persistent discrimination against its Palestinian Arab citizens. Needless to say, one will not find in the literature reviewed any reference to crimes such as the Kufr Qasim massacre, when on the eve of the joint Franco-British-Israeli aggression against Egypt, on 29 October 1956, 49 Palestinian Arabs were murdered in cold blood by Israeli border police units at the entrance to their village.

By projecting this hateful and evil stereotype of the Arab, these authors construct very serious obstacles to the development of any orientation or aspiration towards peace in the minds of their young readers.

The Arab soldiers and officers are portrayed as cruel, not only to the enemy but also to each other. The Arab soldiers are also portrayed as despicable and dishonourable, devoid of respect for their comrades-in-arms, and consequently for the rules of war, let alone for prisoners of war.

> They [The Syrians] bombard our settlements in the north. They send saboteurs to commit acts of sabotage against peaceful farmers, fishermen and workers. They are preparing for the next war and they are fortifying the area . . . We are all aware how they molested our prisoners when they got caught in Syria while on an intelligence mission. They were subjected to cruel torture and one of them committed suicide. Others of our prisoners were kept in jail for long years, and when released many required hospitalisation in mental institutions because they [the Syrian soldiers] despise every law and every regulation regarding prisoners of war and detainees. (Biber 1974:21–2)

How do the authors of this literature illustrate to the young reader the cruelty of the Arab soldier? Let us consider the following narrative about an Israeli pilot who was shot down in Syria on an intelligence mission, and who still, after two years in a Syrian jail, refuses to talk. He is called by General Abdallah of the Syrian army for another interrogation session at which he persists in his refusal to co-operate:

> "Do you know what terrible torture we will subject you to if you do not reveal to us the secret of the aircraft which you invented?" General Abdallah asked him openly.
> "Torture will not make me speak."
> "Show him, Ahmad [one of the General's aides], show him some of our torture implements, a taste of which he will get if he does not talk as I require," roared General Abdallah. Ahmad opened a huge crate and pulled out a giant saw.
> "There is no need to explain to you what is done with this saw," said General Abdallah in a sweet voice. "It saws, very painfully, fingers, arms . . . legs . . ."
> The prisoner remained silent. Ahmad took out a pair of big pincers.
> "Oh pincers," called General Abdallah. "What will you pinch today? Or perhaps it is more correct to ask who will you pinch today? Or better what member and whose member [will you pinch today]? The right ear perhaps? The left? The nose? The tongue? . . ."
> A slight shiver went through the prisoner who was listening in silence. But he did not blink an eyelid. Ahmad took out from the box a giant drill.
> "Hello drill," called General Abdallah. "Who will you drill today? And where will you drill? In the stomach? In the heart? In the throat? In the brain?"
> The prisoner rocked on his feet but his mouth remained locked.
> "You are still silent – eh?" cried General Abdallah in a venomous voice. "Let's see if you will remain silent when we illustrate on you the action of these implements." (Sarig 1968b: 63–5)

This narrative does not depict real torture; it does not need to. It is sufficient to present the implements of torture to the prisoner and supplement the narrative with pictures. This particular book is extensively illustrated and among the illustrations is a picture of giant pincers and a chained person (see Appendix). These implements of torture are not used on the prisoner, not because the Arab officer turns out to be a good or a reasonable man after all, but because of the intervention of Dannidin, the invisible "superman", who rushes to the rescue of the prisoner.

The Arab soldiers and officers are cruel not only to the enemy but also to each other and to their own people. The literature reviewed contains many portrayals of the Arab, frequently Egyptian, officer as stupid and cruel. Consider for instance the following:

The Egyptian officer Abdallah Naftuzi appeared [in the tent of his soldiers] and his black overgrown moustache announced a bad omen. He waved a leather whip in his hand.

"I hear that there is here among our Egyptian soldiers a Jewish boy. Is this correct?"

Henriko's heart froze inside his chest.

"He is my nephew," faltered Hasan.

"He is a spy," screamed Abdallah Naftuzi, "and both of you will be thrown into jail. Tomorrow morning we are attacking the Jews and he came to spy on us and to reveal our plans."

"He is my nephew, I swear by the life of the prophet," lied Hasan in his attempt to save Henriko's life. "He came from Haifa. My brother worked in Haifa and this is my brother's son. I swear by the horse of the prophet."

"Come, come to me you son of impudence," he [Abdallah Naftuzi] screamed at Hasan. "With the whip in my hand I will slash your body until you tell the truth, all the truth . . ."

Abdallah Naftuzi turned to Hasan. "Ya Hasan, you said that this youth is your nephew?"

"Yes indeed, Sir," answered Hasan courageously.

"Then this is my verdict. You will be subjected to ten lashes, terrible lashes from my strong and severe hand. If after the flogging you will repeat and confirm your words, I will judge that you said the truth. And if not, I will judge that you lied." Abdallah Naftuzi twirled his moustache and his eyes lit with the glitter of hatred and cruelty. "Are you willing to suffer a flogging?" he asked with contempt.

He was twenty years old and his entire world was mediocre, confined to discipline and drilling. Those were his soldiers and he despised them wholeheartedly. They were hardworking peasants, whereas he was engrossed in vanity from his youth, and he now became an officer in the army of the Egyptian King.

"I am willing to suffer the flogging," answered Hasan and stepped one step forward.

"Stretch across that bed," ordered the officer.

Hasan stretched himself across the bed with his arms spread out. His shirt and his hat rolled on the floor.

"Is this youth your nephew?"

"He is my nephew."

The whip descended with a whistle on Hasan's back and engraved on it a narrow reddish stripe. Drops of blood began to trickle out of the peasant's flesh.

"Is he your nephew?" repeated Abdallah Naftuzi.

> "Even if you give me one hundred lashes until I die, I will repeat and say, he is my nephew," cried Hasan courageously.
>
> The whip whistled ten times. Ten terrible lashes descended upon the back of the peasant and he did not reveal his secret. Obstinately he repeated and said that Mahmud, namely Henriko, was his relative, a member of his family. (Mosinson 1975: 86–92)

This quote illustrates the extreme stupidity, cruelty and mindlessness of the Arab officer, who wants to expose the truth by flogging his own soldier without even bothering to interrogate the child; without attempting to check or corroborate the truth in any other way. The author, of course, could not allow the officer to talk to the child because as the reader is aware, Hasan is lying and the child is indeed a spy. On the other hand, the author wants to arouse the readers' anger against the Egyptian officer in order to be able to develop the plot in such a manner as to acclimatize them to the war ethos of the book, and lead them to the conclusion that these cruel people deserve all that they get. In the story the author goes out of his way to emphasise that the other soldiers are no better than their officer in that they are jubilant when they see their comrade dripping with blood.

It is interesting to note the manner in which the author chooses to end this part of his narrative.

> "Dog, son of a dog," the officer cursed furiously at Hasan, who was bleeding.
>
> "Dog son of a dog. The issue of miserable *fallahin*. This time you did not lie, but you will of course lie in future. This flogging is an advance. I have yet to see a *fallah* who does not lie or swear in vain. You will yet know the strength of my hand and my judgement." With these words Abdallah Naftuzi took leave of the residents of the tent and went out to seek a new victim from among his miserable soldiers. (Mosinson 1975:92)

The officer is portrayed as despicable, but are his soldiers any better? The reader of course feels pity for Hasan, the poor, good-hearted Egyptian soldier who wants to help Henriko, the little Jewish boy who has crossed the border, but correlatively the narrative carries the message that the officer is, in fact, right. Hasan is a liar and a traitor. He does shelter an Israeli spy, who eventually passes military information to the Israelis. Hasan is thus also portrayed as despicable since he betrays his homeland and his people; cruel, since because of his lying the Israelis succeed in killing many soldiers from among his people.

In other words, both the Arab officer and the Arab soldier are portrayed as the lowest of the low. By whatever terms they be judged, they are devoid of any commitment to human values and conscience. Against this background the Israeli characters emerge as the epitome of logic and morality. An Israeli would never contemplate sheltering a spy; an Israeli would immediately deliver the spy to the authorities.

The Arab officers and soldiers are portrayed consistently throughout the literature as outright idiots. They believe anything said to them. Most authors describe how their Israeli heroes can readily "sell" Arab officers any lie whatsoever simply because the Arabs do not know what is really going on. The following quote illustrates the structure and process of this portrayal. The Israeli heroes have been captured by the Egyptians and are commanded to reveal military secrets in order to save their lives. Note the following exchange:

> "You are very good children, you are sugar children," he said in broken Hebrew and licked his thick lips with his tongue. "I came to see you," opened Sergeant Abu Silwan in a flattering voice," so that you can tell me a little bit of what you know about the army of Israel. Just a few not very important things," he said and smiled sweetly, "and then I will set you free to go home."
> "He thinks we are idiots," whispered fat Ehud to Uzi who stood next to him.
> "You just tell me how many tanks the Israeli army has, how many airplanes and how many soldiers and such similar few unimportant matters and then I will let you go free. Agree?" Sergeant Abu Silwan considered himself to be very clever and believed that the members of Hasambah were foolish children who would be willing to tell all they know in return for a sweet. (Mosinson 1971:83–4)

The children decide to convey to the Egyptian military man "important information on the Israeli army". This information is, of course, nonsense, and they readily succeed in making a fool of the military governor.

> "How many tanks do the Jews have and of what make?" [the officer] asked Yaron, fixing his gaze at him.
> "We have 'Samordin' tanks," answered Yaron (an improvised derivative of the word "sardine". Yaron chose the name because of its Russian sound and because the encounter took place just after the Russian–Egyptian arms deal).
> "Samordin?" wondered the Governor, "I have never heard of a tank of this name."
> "This is because it is our most secret weapon," answered Yaron in great earnestness. "A Samordin tank has 14 guns."
> "Unbelievable," muttered the Governor, "14 guns?! I swear by Mohammad and his noble horse that I had never heard of a tank of the type of Samordin."
> "You must inform your Prime Minister the dictator Abd al-Nasir [Abdul Nasser]. It is very important that he will know of it," Yaron pulled the leg of Sergeant Abu Silwan.
> "And what kind of airplanes do you have?" asked the Governor. "I don't mean ordinary airplanes of the kind that the rest of the world has."
> "Do you therefore mean our secret airplanes?" Yaron pulled the Governor by the tongue.
> "Exactly," said Sergeant Abu Silwan, and he continued to write fast all that Yaron Zehavi told him.
> "We have a very advanced aircraft of the type 'Shut Up Id' (shut up idiot)," said the commander of Hasambah with a flourish.
> "Shut Up Id?" the Governor repeated the name in order to ascertain that he made no mistake.

"Yes, Shut Up Id," confirmed Yaron, pulling one leg over another.

"And how fast is it?" asked the Governor, after noting the name of the aircraft on the piece of paper in front of him.

"2,000 kilometres per hour," answered Yaron. "It is almost as if before it begins its flight it has already completed it. It is so fast that it is completely undetectable."

"Unbelievable," said the Governor holding his head with incredulity. "Shut Up Id, you said? Interesting, very interesting."

"Yes, Shut Up Id," Yaron repeated the name with relish. "The Shut Up Id is a most dangerous aircraft. Our enemies should know that."

"God is the greatest," whispered the Governor in fear. "Abd al-Nasir [Abdul Nasser] is preparing to start a war against Israel, and he does not know at all what is in store for him. God is the greatest."

"Then tell him to stop doing nonsense," volunteered Yaron, "he had once already tasted the taste of the beating of our soldiers. He had better not provoke us again."

"I will phone him immediately," said Sergeant Abu Silwan earnestly. (Mosinson 1971:91–3)

The quote above indicates complete contempt of Arab intelligence. The Arab military governor is portrayed as believing the boy without further questioning or checking the truth of his claims. Later in this story the Israeli boy talks directly to Nasser and warns him.

The literature examined is full of such portrayals. In almost all the books reviewed I found representation of the "idiot" Arab soldier, officer or governor, even Arab rulers. This representation is particularly prevalent in the "Hasambah", "Dannidin" and "Azit" series. In one of these stories Dannidin, the invisible Israeli hero, approaches Gamal Abdul Nasser himself, and slaps him twice on the cheek and then kicks him on his backside. Nasser just stands like an idiot before his officers. The narrative develops as follows:

Nasser, flabbergasted, covered his face with both his hands and immediately got a smashing kick on his backside.

"Oy!" he shouted, and immediately turned around and shot his fist in the face of Sergeant Hasan, who stood very excited behind him. Hasan of course did not dare to hit back.

"Put him in jail," Nasser issued an order to his officers. "Did you not see that he slapped me on the face from the back and kicked me? He is insane."

"Yes, I am completely insane," said Hasan, agreeing vigorously.

The Egyptians were educated to agree to anything that Nasser says, even if the statement were completely stupid. (Sarig 1968a:85-6)

The Arab soldiers are further portrayed as cowards throughout the literature reviewed. Arab soldiers and officers are both portrayed as being of poor fighting morale; they abandon the battlefield without fighting; one round of bullets is sufficient to chase them away. Cowardice is presented as part of the Arab character. This further intensifies contempt for the Arab, and accentuates the positive qualities of the Israeli "superman".

> He [the Jewish boy] hardly noticed what he was doing. He shifted his Uzi submachine gun slightly and fired a short round which scraped a few millimetres over the head of the Arab policeman but did not hit him. This was sufficient. The astonished Arab turned back and fled for his life. (Ofeq 1969a: 62)

The following narrative is spoken by an Israeli Jew who is sharing stories of his heroism in the battle of the occupation of Beersheba in the 1948 war.

> And then the Egyptian commander cried: "Don't shoot! don't shoot!" "Raise your hands," I shouted at him.
> The fat Egyptian Commander raised his hands and came out of the police building followed by his Deputy who was slightly less fat, and behind them all the rest of the officers. The process stretched over a full five minutes, until all the officers came out, fifty, sixty perhaps; rubbish, fifty or sixty, one hundred officers were there and we were altogether 10 soldiers in a troop carrier. After the officers, the soldiers begin to appear: ten, twenty, fifty, a hundred, one hundred and fifty . . . After a quarter of an hour there were outside perhaps some three hundred Egyptians, and they were still coming out. When the Egyptian officer realised that we were only 10 people there were strange signs in his eyes. (Nadel 1974: 38, 39)

Three hundred people, maybe more, are not willing to fight. They simply come out of the police building. Opposite them stand ten Israelis who are of course "supermen". This portrayal of Arab soldiers and officers is an essential part of Israeli youth education. Its object is to communicate the allegation that Arabs cannot fight against Israelis.

Worse narratives fill the pages of the children's stories reviewed, including the extract given below which depicts Arab soldiers, in this case Egyptian soldiers, not only fleeing from battle but also abandoning their boots in the process: this myth of the Egyptian Arab soldier abandoning his boots features in all Israeli portrayals of Arab fighting with the exception of the 1973 war. Pictures were printed by all Israeli papers of the heaps of boots which the Egyptians abandoned in their flight from the battlefield. (There is some evidence to indicate that the contrary is the truth: Egyptian prisoners of war were forced by the Israeli army to take off their boots, and were then ordered to trek back to Egypt barefoot through the desert. In desert conditions, this is almost tantamount to a verdict of mass murder. See, for instance, ISRAC, No. 2, March 1970, which gives a photograph of Egyptian POWs in the June 1967 war being forced at gunpoint by Israeli soldiers to take off their boots in the scorching (160°F) desert sand. Israeli propaganda spread the story that the Egyptian soldiers ran away leaving their boots behind.)

> The scenery turned to desert. All around lay the expanses of sand bearing the furrows of car wheels. Throughout there were scattered numerous boots, which drew the attention of the children. "These belong to the Egyptians," explained the father. "In their terrified flight they took off their boots and

escaped barefoot. Across the desert there are thousands of abandoned military boots many of which are officers' boots." (Oren 1964:20)

Lying and exaggeration are similarly portrayed as part of the character of the Arab soldier and officer. These features are most prominent and are a marked contrast to those of the Israeli fighter.

General Abdallah stood before the large mirror in the command room of the Nuqayb fortress. His chest was decorated with many glittering "medals" and he viewed himself with open admiration. "Well, my attaché Ahmad," he turned to his new attaché, "what do you say about my new decorations of excellence?"

"They are wonderful, General Abdallah," hastened the attaché Ahmad to reply. "I have yet to see a General in the Syrian army or a Commander of a fortress in Syria who has so many and so exalted decorations of excellence."

"Let me explain to you, Ahmad, how I came to get them," said the General. "The supreme decoration for valour is given, as you know, in recognition of supreme valour at the time of assault against the enemy. The supreme decoration of courage is given, as you know, in recognition of putting one's life at risk on behalf of the homeland in the face of enemy attack. The decoration of excellent service is given in recognition of most efficient organization of attack against the enemy, and the decoration of conquest and victory is given in recognition of the conquest of a large enemy position."

"But Commander, forgive my ignorance, I do not recall that we had ever conquered any large enemy position. How is it, if I may ask, Commander, that you have won these decorations and especially the decoration of conquest and victory?" asked the attaché Ahmad hesitantly.

"Very simple," roared at him General Abdallah. "I will yet conquer a large enemy position when we come out again, one day soon, in war against Israel. So of what importance is it if I wear the decoration of conquest and victory before the conquest or after? It is certain isn't it that I will conquer a large Israeli position. Right?"

"Of course General Abdallah, of course," hastened attaché Ahmad to confirm. The General proceeded with pleasure pointing to his various other decorations of excellence. "To the decoration of supreme valour I am entitled in recognition of three Israeli tanks which I shall eliminate with my own hands," said General Abdallah. "I will eliminate them when I conquer the large Israeli position in recognition of which I am entitled to the decoration of conquest and victory. As to the decoration of supreme courage, this I am entitled to have in recognition of killing 20 Israeli soldiers all by myself, in face to face combat, during their counter-attack to regain the position, which I will conquer from them, and the decoration of excellent service I received in recognition of the excellent organization of the attack, which I will launch against the position. Do all these decorations of excellence suit me Ahmad?"

"They suit you very well General Abdallah; they are very beautiful," hastened Ahmad to reassure him, "and I am confident that you will succeed to do all that you said you would." (Sarig 1968b: 25–8)

By way of summary, it is evident that the image of the Arab soldier and officer as portrayed in the literature reviewed does not invite any respect.

Quite the contrary, it is intended to invite contempt. They are cowardly, spineless, weak and devoid of values. They are portrayed as liars, and their lies are intended to cover up their weakness and defeat. The general impression conveyed is that the Arab fighter is inferior to the Israeli soldier, the latter repeatedly demonstrating his power as a "superman".

I did not locate in the books reviewed for this research any attempt whatsoever to present an analysis of the Arab fighter. None of the authors decided to present an ideological or social account of the thoughts of these people. The Arab soldier and officer are portrayed as lacking any regard for their homeland and as totally unaware of the reason for fighting. The only motivation ascribed to them is "the Arab hatred of the Jews". Yet despite their hatred the Arabs have no choice but to fear and respect the Israelis.

The Arab soldier is presented as an idiot who is willing to accept anything said by his commander. He has no opinion of his own, not even in matters non-military. All the authors reviewed seem to make every effort to reduce the human value of the Arab soldier; sometimes they communicate the feeling that nothing much will be lost if the persons concerned disappear.

The Arab officer is portrayed as imbecilic and cruel. He is very much concerned with his appearance; always polished; usually moustached; fat; he carries a whip in his hand; shouts; never laughs; is always right, never willing to accept any comment regarding any of his decisions, even when they are obviously extremely stupid. He despises his soldiers, treats them with manifest disregard, and addresses them in humiliating terms.

In contrast the same authors, in every case, portray the Israeli soldier and officer in exactly opposite terms. The juxtaposition is so mechanical that one could take each of the constitutive elements of the image of the Arab soldier and officer, and illustrate how the image of the Israeli is constituted by the contrary reference: courageous; of high fighting morale; responsible; liberal; truthful; thoughtful; wise.

I found a significant difference, however, between the portrayal of the Egyptian fighter and the Syrian fighter. The image of the Egyptian invites no respect. He is always cowardly, stupid and devoid of self-respect. But it seems that hatred for the Egyptian soldier and officer, as expressed in the literature reviewed, is less than the hatred for his Syrian counterpart, who invites much greater respect throughout the literature. Almost without exception, the Syrian soldier is shown in combat, never laughing or playing cards. The description above of the Syrian officer making a fool of himself by indulging in fantastic wishful thinking is highly exceptional. Generally, it is the Syrian soldier who is associated with combat and torture – not the Egyptian.

In some of the stories reviewed there are references to Iraqi, Lebanese and Saudi soldiers but these are marginal and negligible for our purposes. There are also references to Jordanian soldiers, and one can discern a significant distinction between the portrayal of the Syrian soldier and the Jordanian soldier. Interestingly, the Jordanian soldier is portrayed as a good and serious fighter though of course not as wise and strong as the Israelis.

The 1973 War

One would expect the impact of successive Israeli–Arab wars, in 1948, 1956, 1967 and 1973, to be reflected in the literature, and that following each of these major events in the history of the state of Israel some modification of the image of the Arab to be made. But until 1973 the image of the Arab remained essentially static and unaltered. The 1973 war, however, did effect a significant change, though not directly in the image of the Arab soldier and officer; rather in the correlative image of the Israeli soldier. For the first time in the wake of the 1973 war there appear references in the literature to dead Israeli soldiers, burnt Israeli tents and Israeli soldiers abandoning their positions. This is unprecedented prior to the 1973 war. Until then the Israelis were always the heroes and the victors.

In most of the literature produced in the immediate wake of the 1973 war the plot and narrative are located in the fighting on the Golan Heights, the northeastern front. I did not locate any literature plotted against the backdrop of the southern Israeli–Egyptian front. In my view the reason for this could be the important difference in the fortunes of the Israeli army during the 1973 war on the northern front from on the southern front. In the northeastern front, although the Syrian army succeeded in overrunning Israeli defence positions and settlements in the Golan Heights in the first days of the war, the Israeli army successfully mounted a counter-attack and reoccupied the major portion of the lost territory. In the southern front, on the other hand, the Egyptian army succeeded not only in crossing the Suez Canal, destroying the Bar Lev defence line and occupying the eastern bank of the Canal, but more significantly, the Israeli army failed in all of its attempts to dislodge the Egyptian troops. The successful penetration of the Israeli army into Egyptian territory from behind the front line is only tangentially relevant in this context. The majority of the Golan Heights still remains under Israeli occupation (the territory was officially annexed in 1981), whereas through a succession of disengagement agreements culminating in the Camp David Accords of 1978 and the Israeli–Egyptian peace treaty of 1979, the entire Egyptian Sinai Peninsula was returned to Egyptian sovereignty. The regional power balance altered following the 1973 war, entailing in the southern front an irreducible territorial loss, from the Israeli point of view. It is hardly conceivable for any narrative to be plotted against the backdrop of the 1973 war in the southern front without reference to this political consequence. It is not possible to veil the Israeli territorial defeat in the southern front, whereas, on the northeastern front, the successful Israeli counter-attack and reoccupation did constitute a territorial victory. I submit that it is predominantly this consideration which explains why in the post-1973 literature under review all the books, with only one exception, refer only to the 1973 war against the Syrian army and the recapture of the Golan territory.

Everything is already behind us. Everything. The evacuation; the shells; the fire; the fear; and again we need to begin here anew. To become the "people of the beginning". . . And this we shall do. Soon nobody will recognize what happened here. Our farm will be like before the war. The irises will flower under the window; the hens cackle in the coop and awaken me from my sleep. Father will go out to the farm (he is a real herder, my father) and mother will receive visitors and serve them cakes. I will go out to the orchard to see if the peaches are ripened . . . Yes I'm certain: anyone who will visit here soon will not discern at all what was and what happened here between Yom Kippur and Simhat Torah; will recognize almost nothing. Just the remnants of a deserted outpost; a small crater scarring the big rock and perhaps an empty shell case in the valley opposite. (Ofek 1974:7)

Nevertheless the authors could not completely disregard the effect of the war on Israeli Jewish society. Something happened to the soul of the Israeli Jew. For the first time the fear and the confusion of the Israeli Jew appears in the literature:

"It began".
  These were probably the first two words that crossed my mind but there was no time for further thought. For one short moment, or maybe one long moment, I stood paralysed, my legs trembling, my eyes roving all over the place, watching how the terrible war is alighting all around. A line of tanks begins to move slowly, slowly over the distant plain with the barrels of the cannons directed towards the observation post, and perhaps also against other posts. The middle barrel, so it seemed to me, was aimed directly at me. A long whistle of a shell cuts through the sky high above me. At first it is faint and distant, and after one second it becomes sharp, sending a shiver along one's body and forcing one to stoop one's head. Then it moves further away to the West and ends in a thunderous thud and a strange silence. The noise of the jets passes above my head. A formation of four MIG aircraft cuts through the sky at terrible speed towards Mount Hermon. A terrible noise engulfs me and it increases more and more. I never imagined that there is in the world such terrifying noise, so frightening that for a minute it seemed to be as if I were a little grain ground between huge millstones; as if the land is trembling under me and I will soon fall into a deep and black pit. (Ofek 1974:60-1)

Such a narrative was inconceivable in books published prior to the 1973 war. Then the Israeli Jew was always confident that any Arab military action against Israel would be immediately countered, and there was therefore no ground for fear or anxiety. For the Israeli Jew prior to 1973 it was inconceivable that the Arab soldier would change and that it was now within his capacity to initiate a war, and advance and occupy Israeli territory.

"We must descend to the shelter," said Danni. "We must run fast before we are hit by one of these," and he pointed towards the shell crater and grabbed Uri's arm.
  I caressed the coat of Saar [the dog]. "I think that all of this is nothing," I said with assurance. "Very soon our aircraft will come and show them. You

must understand, Danni, that here in the Golan Heights we are used to such incidents."

But Danni was not convinced. "Used or not used," he said, "everyone goes down to the shelters."

I laughed. "Let them go down," I said. "I am remaining outside. I will not miss the aircraft, I must see them swoop." (Ron-Feder 1974: 8)

The child waits outside for the Israeli aircraft to sweep through the sky. He wants to see active Israeli retaliation. He waits and indeed an aircraft does appear in the sky.

I had barely finished and on the horizon an aircraft was seen advancing towards us. Meanwhile also Hemdah, the communal child-minder of Uri's group, approached us and urged us to hurry: what do we mean standing like that in the middle of the field as if nothing had happened. Did we not see or hear the exploding shell?

"We did see," I answered impatiently, and followed intently the approaching aircraft. "Look up, soon this pilot will show them who we are."

But to my misfortune I was wrong. The string of bombs fired from the aircraft at us made me realize my mistake. Hemdah shot towards us and threw herself flat on the ground. Uri shrank his body and buried his head in his hands. Also Danni flattened himself on the ground, whereas I threw myself at Saar's back to protect him from the shrapnel, as I saw in the films. I admit I shivered with fear. The bombs fired by the aircraft fell really close to us, and it was only a miracle that we were saved. Saar whined, Hemdah rose from the ground, looked anxiously right and left, and ordered: Quickly to the shelter. (Ron–Feder 1974:9)

A new element that emerges in the post-1973 narrative is the order to evacuate. Until 1973 it was axiomatic in the Zionist context that any Hebrew settlement established on land considered the land of Israel would not be evacuated or removed. The order of evacuation is correctly presented as arousing incredulous shock:

My father directed his surprised and confused look at the uncalled for visitor. I have never seen him so uncertain. "You want to tell me that there is an order to evacuate Neot Golan? Well, for your information I did not come here in order to get evacuated. I . . ."

"Not only Neot Golan. All the settlements along the border are being evacuated."

"But this does not stand to reason," said my father and began dressing.

"Stands to reason or does not stand to reason, this is an order" said the messenger, and I noticed that he was beginning to lose patience. (Ofek 1974:56

Or similarly:

"Three settlements received orders of evacuation," whispered Noah's mother into Hemdah's ear. But because I was lying very close to them I could hear the whisper as well.

"What?" Hemdah was flabbergasted.

"Exactly what you hear," said Noah's mother. "We received the order on our communication radio. By noon they have to leave the place . . ."

But . . ."

Noah's mother smiled. "Yes," she said, trembling somewhat. "Also they said, 'but': it did not help them. This is an order from above. It seems that serious war is taking place there." (Ron-Feder 1974: 12)

One of the new dimensions introduced into the literature in the wake of the 1973 war is this dimension of incredulity. The Israeli Jews could not believe what their ears heard and what their eyes saw, namely, that the Arabs are really capable of fighting, occupying land, hitting Israeli tanks and shooting down Israeli airplanes.

"What will happen if Syrian soldiers enter here first?" asked Limor.

But Boaz said that that was impossible. Rubbish, Syrian soldiers. He was ready to bet on his head that within an hour or so our armour will chase away the Syrian tanks and within a day or two we go back home. (Ron-Feder 1974: 19)

And similarly:

My class huddled together in the new shelter at the centre of the settlement. We were ordered to enter and get ourselves settled for a long stay. We were not used to that. In the previous war after the sounding of the siren, we entered the shelters for a short while and then we went out and roamed around all corners of the yard. Now it was necessary to find some way to pass the time. They say that time is dear when scarce, but it is like a used coin when there is nothing to do with it. (Epstein 1975: 25)

As indicated above, the authors attempted to veil from the young reader the fact that the 1973 war showed an important change in the performance of the Arab soldier. On the other hand this new development could not be completely denied since every child and every adult in Israel knew that this war was different from any other war. Arab leaders have always been accused by the Israeli media of hiding "the truth" from their people, especially in time of war or other catastrophe. In the 1973 war it transpired that this was not an exclusive failure of the Arab leadership, but that the Israeli leadership was guilty of the same omission. This came as a shock to the majority of Israeli Jews. This shock is reflected in the literature under review.

One evening when the war was at its zenith we held a conversation in the children's society on the course of the war. A veteran member who was active in the [pre-1948] Palmah stormtroops and is now active in security matters of the settlement, gave us a review of the situation, as far as it could be assessed, and also answered questions.

We wanted to know what was happening at the front. How was it that we were taken by surprise and what were the odds? Someone among us asked: "During the Six Days War there was no television and still we knew each day very clearly what the Israeli army did that day. Each evening or late at night the radio gave reports on the achievements. We were then kindergarten pupils, but we knew then much much more than we know now. The television does show us scenes on the progress of war, but how do we stand? What are we to expect?" (Epstein 1975: 33)

The answer of the former Palmah activist, subsequently in charge of the security affairs of the settlement, is vague and unconvincing to the children. It is as though intended to tell them that it is not important whether or not they know exactly what is going on. All he can suggest is that they rely on the Israeli army.

The Israeli army is not groping in the dark. If it is silent it is surely because it is forbidden to communicate moves or results that could be of benefit to the enemy. Our army now stands back on its feet again and this will soon be felt. (Epstein 1975: 34)

Until 1973 the authors of the literature under review generally disregarded the question of Israeli casualties. The Israeli soldier had always won wars without casualties, in true "superman" fashion. The 1973 war changed that: it was no longer possible to disregard the question:

"Are you wounded?"
"No, thank God, no."
"This smell," his voice trembled . . . "The blood is Moshik's. He was killed. I tried to treat his wound but I did not succeed . . . Also the others were killed. Six of our tanks arrived to defend the Kibbutz and none of the tank teams remained alive except myself." (Ron-Feder 1974:82-4)

It is my reasoned view that despite all efforts to the contrary, in the wake of the 1973 war the young readership developed a new image of the Arab fighter. This image was informed by the knowledge that in the 1973 war the Arabs demonstrated that they could fight, occupy and kill, destroy Israeli tanks and shoot down Israeli aircraft. It remains for subsequent research to examine the long-term effects of this change on commercial Israeli Hebrew children's story-books.

8. Conclusion

In order to consolidate its colonial ideology, the Zionist movement has found it necessary to reduce and destroy the image of the Palestinian Arab. This is reflected in the commercial Israeli Hebrew children's literature which is the subject matter of this study. The overwhelming majority of the books written on life in Palestine before the establishment of the state of Israel portray the country as empty of population and emphasize through long passages of indoctrination that it belongs to the Jews. Jewish ownership of the land of Palestine is invariably related to the Bible or biblical Jewish history.

The theme of Jewish ownership is presented most radically through the mouth of the "positive" Arab who explains to the child readers that Palestine indeed belongs to the Jews, and that the Arabs really have no rights over the land, or alternatively that Arabs began to migrate there only after the Jewish community began to establish itself in the country.

The small minority of authors who have attempted to address the problem in different terms, and present the argument that the Arabs too have the right to live in the country, have always and without exception been forced by their underlying Zionist commitment to come out with the conclusion that though the country, Palestine, belongs only to Jews, the Arabs may live there under Jewish rule.

The young Jewish readership of this literature receives only one explanation for the protracted conflict: the Arab is motivated by his desire to kill the Jews, steal their property and expel them from their homeland. The development of this theme and the correlative image of the Arab as a backward and dangerous native who must be civilized are therefore inherent in the colonial situation. The literature reviewed thus presents the war between Jews and Arabs in Palestine as a war between good (the Jew) and evil (the Arab). The Jew aims to build, the Arab aims to destroy. The Arab must therefore be removed, destroyed or neutralized in order to protect the good from the evil. Nowhere in the literature is there even the slightest mention that the lands on which Jewish cities and agricultural settlements were established belonged in reality to the Arabs, the same Arabs who were removed from them and who now attack those who dispossessed them. In order to lend credibility to the argument, special emphasis is laid on the Arab bedouins. They are given an unreal and extraordinary image, deliberately fabricated in an attempt to reduce the Palestinian Arab society into one that has no real attachment to the land: a nomad society of bedouins. After effecting such a reduction it becomes possible to "prove" that Palestine was indeed empty of population. It is characteristic of the bedouins that they are both present and non-present; they exist and yet they are not there.

The literature exhibits strong emphasis on Jewish progress: the Jew is mechanized; his agricultural tool is the tractor, whereas the Arab is backward; his agricultural tool is the plough. The Jew maintains the countryside, whereas the Arab destroys it. The Jew aims to establish new settlements; the Arab aims to destroy them for no reason whatever. The Jew dresses like a "civilized" European, whereas the Arab dress is primitive, exotic at best. The Jew wants to live in peace; the Arab wants to rob and murder.

In this context the image of the "positive", "good" Arab is central. The good Arab is the one who accepts Zionist assumptions and is willing to confront his own people in the defence of Zionist objectives. Significantly, there is no parallel image of the positive or good Jew who would have to be a traitor. The good Jew is portrayed as the Jew who wishes to live in peace in the country on the condition that Arabs accept Zionist terms of reference. He is willing to go even further and recognize that Palestine belongs to two peoples, but one people fled; therefore the remaining people, the Israeli Jewish people, are not responsible for the tragedy of the other, the Palestinian Arab people. The good Jew is a Jew who takes pity on the Arabs and who wishes to solve the problems of the Palestinian Arab people on the condition that they do not live inside the state of Israel. The good Jew is the Jew who desires to teach the Arabs, to free the Arab peoples from their dictators, and live in peace with the Arab nations, on condition that they disregard the injustice inflicted on the Palestinian Arab people.

This image of the good Jew reflects the reality of Jewish colonial existence in Palestine. The Jew in Palestine could not establish himself as the White in America did: the White in America annihilated the entire American Indian society, whereas the Palestinian Arab resistance to the Jewish colonial enterprise was more successful and did not allow this to happen. Neither could the Jews in Palestine establish themselves like the Whites in southern Africa, again largely because the Palestinian Arab resistance did not allow them to. The result is a person (the Jew) who consistently lies, yet is convinced that he or she does not lie; consistently distorts, yet is convinced that he or she does not distort; a person who desires to present before the public clean hands, and yet his or her hands are dipped in blood and the robbery of the Palestinian Arab people's homeland. Needless to say, this image of the good Jew articulates a deep insight into the contingencies of Zionist morality and ideology.

The Arab character as presented in the children's literature under review is horrific. Central to the presentation of the Arab character is a radical generalization: all Arabs are corrupt; all are willing to commit any action, including treason, for money; all Arabs swear; all Arabs are physically and mentally filthy; all Arabs dress funnily and cover their heads with a kerchief like women, etc . . . Conversely, all Jews are honourable, incorruptible, civilized, clean, and Western. Needless to say, Jews never swear . . . The same structure underlies the presentation of the Palestinian Arab fighter. The Palestinian Arab fighter fights only because he is part of an incited mob. He does not know why and what he is fighting for. His fighting has no ideological motive. At best he fights in order to kill and loot, or in order to appropriate Jewish women.

This is in broad outline the image of the Palestinian Arab fighter before the establishment of the state of Israel in 1948. After that date the same person is redefined as an "infiltrator" whose object is still theft, murder and destruction. And after the 1967 war the same person is redefined as a "saboteur". The line of progression is clear: the Palestinian Arab fighter as portrayed in this literature has "developed" from a "murderer" to an "infiltrator" to a "saboteur", and in the most recent version, to a terrorist involved with international crime.

It is important to note that no significant change can be detected in any of the characters' constituent elements throughout the period under review. Major events such as the establishment of the state of Israel in 1948 and the subsequent wars of 1956, 1967 and 1973 did not significantly affect the constitution of this image except in name. The character and motivation remain unaltered.

Dr Adir Cohen, chairman of the Department of Education at the University of Haifa, completed in 1976 detailed research on the image of the Arab in Israeli Hebrew children's literature. His conclusions correspond to the findings of this study.

> The findings must cause concern for education in the country, because it was in this way that the image of the Jew was presented in anti-Semitic Christian literature . . .
> It is amazing to realize that over the long years of common life between Jews and Arabs, no change can be detected in the attitude [to the Arab]. There is no attempt in the literature to relate to the Arabs as equals. (*Ha'aretz,* 30 June 1976)

The constancy of the image of the Arab in the literature reviewed, unrelated to and unaffected by concrete material and political changes to life in Palestine and Israel throughout the period under study, can be understood only in relation to the nature of political Zionism as a racialist and colonialist movement. The image of the Arab is constant because it relates to a central element at the heart of Zionist ideology, namely Jewish supremacy. There is little reason to believe, given historical precedents, that racialist philosophy can be reformed from within the society structured around it. Historically such philosophies have been reformed largely by external intervention. The French colonial society in Algeria did not voluntarily reform its ethical philosophy. It paid dearly for the reform, as did the Algerian Arab people. The same applies to South Africa and the same is likely to apply in Palestine.

I wish to end this concluding chapter with a comment on the standard of the books and their illustrations.

The standard of the books, with very rare exceptions, is extremely low. Very few of the authors attempt to deal with the subject of the Arab in any depth, even from an anti-Arab perspective. The books are superficial. They address the emotions and the prejudice of the reader, very rarely his or her intellect. Nor do the majority of the authors allow the reader the opportunity to think or develop his or her own conclusion. No ambiguity is allowed. All answers are presented in detail, and every detail is always fully elucidated. Between the two poles of the completely unrealistic image of the Jew and the similarily unrealistic image of the Arab, the reader is consistently removed from reality.

The books reviewed in the framework of this study were selected because they deal centrally with the Israeli–Arab or Jewish–Arab conflict. Needless to say, the Jew or the Israeli Jew is invariably the victor; the Arabs are always guilty of any injustice perpetrated in Palestine, while the Jew always acts in self-defence.

Most of the books are cheap adventure books. The best-selling series of "Hasambah", "Dannidin" and "The Children of the Old City" seem intended to develop false perceptions in the child readers, based on a distorted sense of reality. There are a number of noted exceptions: the writings of the authors Eliezer Semoli, Uriel Ofek, Galilah Ron-Feder, Binyamin Tamuz, Yehudah Salu and Karah Feder. They seem able to deal with the Jewish–Arab and Israeli–Arab conflict in terms with which I personally disagree, but which are of a high literary standard. Yet for the majority of the authors, the question of peace is always incidental and superficial. It is never centrally discussed because this would entail some discussion of Zionist ideology. When the prospects for peace are raised, the presentation invariably assumes that the Arabs must accept Zionist assumptions and Israeli conditions in order for peace to be established.

The illustrations accompanying the text of the books reviewed correspond to the basic structures of the narrative. The standards are low: the illustrations are shocking in their thorough racism. They underline visually the consistent conceptual stereotype developed in the narrative.

The Palestinian Arab and Israeli Jewish peoples are destined to live together, unless one destroys the other, and that, as I have already noted, is not only ethically unacceptable, but also practically impossible in the 20th century. It is therefore imperative to promote education towards a common life based on equality of rights, and it is important that this educational reform should figure centrally in children's literature. Such a reform must be mutual. I did not in the framework of this study examine Palestinian Arab children's literature or the image of the Jew that this literature presents. It is my hope that Palestinian Arab literature is superior to Israeli Jewish literature in this respect. I consider this study to be a critical contribution towards educational reform in the children's literature of both peoples, and as such, a contribution to the development of a more peaceful relationship between the Palestinian Arab and Jewish peoples in the country.

Bibliography

(H = Hebrew; A = Arabic)

Abu-Lughod, Ibrahim *The Transformation of Palestine* (Northwestern University Press, Evanston, III., 1971).

Adar, L. and Adler, C. *Value Education in Schools for New Immigrant Children* (Hebrew University, School of Education, Jerusalem, 1965).

Al-Abid, Ibrahim *Guide for the Palestine Problem: Questions and Answers* (Palestine Research Center, Beirut, 1969). (A)

Al-Abid, Lutfi and Anza, Musa (translators) *Zionist Thought: Basic Documents* (Palestine Books Series, No. 21, Palestine Research Center, Beirut, 1970). (A)

Al-Azm, Sadiq Jalal *Leftist Studies on the Palestinian Problem* (Dar al-Tali'a lil-Tiba'a wa-al-Nashr, Beirut, 1970). (A)

Alkalai, Yehudah *Collected Works* (Jerusalem, 1945). (H)

Allen, Richard *Imperialism and Nationalism in the Fertile Crescent* (Oxford University Press, London, 1974).

Allush, Naji *Arab Resistance in Palestine 1917–1948* (Dar al-Tali'a, Beirut, 1970 (2nd printing)). (A)

Amun *et al., Palestinian-Arabs in Israel: Two Case Studies* (Ithaca Press, London, 1977).

Bar-Adon, Pesah *Horses Tell the Story* (Am Oved, Tel Aviv, 1966). (H)

Bein, Alex, *Theodor Herzl: A Bibliography* (The Zionist Library, Jerusalem, 1961.) (H)

Belkind, Israel *The Arabs Who Are in the Land of Israel* (Hermon, Jerusalem, 1969 (1st edn, 1928)). (H)

Ben Elissar, Eliyahu *The Diplomacy of the Third Reich and the Jews 1933–1939* (Idanim, Yediot Aharonot, Jerusalem, 1978). (H)

Ben-Gurion, David *Towards the Clarification of the Origin of the Fallahin* (Akhiever, New York, 1917); reprinted in Belkind, Israel *The Arabs Who Are in the Land of Israel* (Herman, Jerusalem, 1969). (H)

—— *Israel: A Personal History* (Funk and Wagnalls, New York, Sabrah Books, New York and Tel Aviv, 1971). (H)

Benni, Margalit *The Son of the Sheikh* (Sifrei Qarni, Tel Aviv, 1958). (H)

Berelson, Bernard *Content Analysis in Communication Research* (Free Press, Glencoe, III., 1952).

Biber, Yehoash *The Adventures of the Reconnaissance Unit Rimon* (Am Oved, Tel Aviv, 1974). (H)

Bober, Arie (ed.) *The Other Israel: The Radical Case against Zionism* (Anchor Books, Doubleday, New York, 1972).

Booth, John Nicholas "The Moral Case for the Arabs", *The Middle East Newsletter,* London , September 1969.

Borochov, *Selected Works,* Editor, Zalman Robashov (Am Oved, Tel Aviv, 1954).

Borochov, Dov Ber *Towards the Question of Zion and Territory* (Am Oved, Tel Aviv, 1954). (H)

Bowle, John *Viscount Samuel* (Victor Gollancz, London, 1957).

Brawer, Abraham Jacob "The Jewish Element in the Arabs of the Land of Israel", *Molad,* New Series,May 1967–May 1968. (H)

Burnstein-Lazar, Tamar *The Adventures of Suleiman and Danni Beyond the Border* (Tsabar Books, Tel Aviv, 1968). (H)

Cauthen, Nelson Robinson, Ira and Krauss, Herbert "Stereotypes: A Review of Literature, 1926–1968", *Journal of Social Psychology,* 1971, pp. 84, 103, 125.

Chernowitz, Yemimah *One of Us* (N. Teverski, Tel Aviv, 1960 (5th edn)). (H)

Childers, Erskine "The Other Exodus", *The Spectator,* London, 12 May 1961, pp. 672–5.

Cohen, Aharon *Israel and the Arab World* (Sifriyat Po'alim, Merhaviyah). (H)

Danni, A. *The Independence of Israel* (Niv, Tel Aviv, 1958). (H)

Davis, Uri *Israel – Utopia Incorporated: A Study of Class, State and Corporate Kin Control* (Zed Press, London, 1977).

Davis, Uri and Lehn, Walter "And the Fund Is Still Alive: The Role of the Jewish National Fund in the Determination of Israel's Settlement Policies", *Journal of Palestine Studies,* Vol. VII, No. 4, 1978.

Davis, Uri, Mack, Andrew and Yuval-Davis, Nira (eds), *Israel and the Palestinians* (Ithaca Press, London, 1975).

Davis, Uri and Mezvinsky, Norton (eds.) *Documents from Israel 1967–1973: Readings for a Critique of Zionism* (Ithaca Press, London, 1975).

Dominitz, Zeev *Baptism of Fire* (Yizra'el, Tel Aviv, 1956). (H)

Ehrlich, Howard *The Social Psychology of Prejudice* (John Wiley & Sons, New York, 1973).

El-Asmar, Fouzi *To Be an Arab in Israel* (Institute for Palestine Studies, Beirut, 1978).

Eliav, Haim *The Children of the Old City Are Fighting Infiltrators* (Niv, Tel Aviv, 1955). (H)

—— *The Children of the Old City and the Treasure of Baghdad* (Yesod, Tel Aviv, 1975a). (H)

—— *The Children of the Old City in Captivity of the Legion* (Yesod, Tel Aviv, 1975b). (H)

—— *The Children of the Old City in the Siege* (Yesod, Tel Aviv, 1975c). (H)

—— *The Children of the Old City Sink a Ship* (Yesod, Tel Aviv, 1975d). (H)

Elon, Amos *The Israelis: Founders and Sons* (Bantam Books/Holt, New York, 1971).

Eppel, M. (ed.) *Education for Cultural Pluralism* (World Jewish Congress, London, 1972).

Epstein, Ben Zion *A Tear in the Bitter Lake* (Etgar, Tel Aviv, 1975). (H)
Faris, Hani "Israel Zangwill's Challenge to Zionism", *Journal of Palestine Studies,* Vol. IV, No. 3, 1975.
Feder, Karah *Let Us Make Peace* (Massadah, Tel Aviv, 1964).
Friedman, Isaiah *Germany, Turkey and Zionism 1897–1918* (Clarendon Press, Oxford, 1977).
Gal, Binyamin *The Foxes of Samson* (Newman, Tel Aviv, 1958). (H)
Goldenberg, Musa *And the Fund Is Still Alive* (Sifriyat Po'alim, Merhaviyah, 1965). (H)
Gordon, Aharon David *Collected Works* (Zionist Books Publications, Jerusalem, 1952–54). (H)
Gur, Motah *Azit in the Desert of Judea* (Yediot Aharonot, Tel Aviv, no date). (H)
—— *Azit the Paratroop Bitch* (Yediot Aharonot, Tel Aviv, 1963). (H)
—— *Azit in the Palaces of Cairo* (Yediot Aharonot, Tel Aviv, 1971). (H)
Gurvitz, Yehudah and Navon, Shemuel (eds) *What Story Will I Tell My Child?* (Amihai, Tel Aviv, 1953). (H)
Ha-Am, Ahad *Collected Works* (Devir. Tel Aviv, 1965). (H)
Halevi, Binyamin *Uri and Ra'anan* (Yavneh, Tel Aviv, 1971). (H)
Hertzberg, Arthur (ed.) *The Zionist Idea: A Historical Analysis and Reader* (A Temple Book, Atheneum, New York, 1976).
Herzl, Theodor *The Complete Diaries of Theodor Herzl* ed Raphael Patai (Herzl Press and Thomas Yoseloff, New York and London, 1960a) (5 volumes).
—— *Old-New Land (Altneuland)* (trans. Lotta Levinsohn (Black Publishing and Herzl Press, New York, 1960b)).
—— *The Jewish State: An Attempt at a Modern Solution of the Jewish Question* (H. Pordes, London, 1967).
International Encyclopaedia of Social Science (Macmillan & Co. and the Free Press, London, 1968).
Israel Pocket Library *Zionism* (Keter Publishing House, Jerusalem, 1973).
Israel Yearbook, 1966–67.
Jiryis, Sabri *The Arabs in Israel* (Monthly Review Press, New York and London, 1976).
—— *A History of Zionism (Vol. I): 1862–1917* (Palestine Research Center, Beirut, 1977).
Jones, Christina *The Untempered Wind: Forty Years in Palestine* (Longman Publishers, London, 1975).
Kafkafi, Eyal "A Ghetto Attitude in the Jewish State", *Davar* (the official daily of the Histadrut (General Federation of Workers in the Land of Israel)), 6 September 1979.
Karmeli, Abner *The Young Sportsmen: Israel against Egypt* (M. Mizrahi, Tel Aviv, 1963). (H)
—— *The Special Reconnaissance* (M. Mizrahi, Tel Aviv, 1971). (H)
—— *The Special Reconnaissance Unit Is Surrounded* (M. Mizrahi, Tel Aviv, 1973).
—— *The Young Sportsmen Return* (M. Mizrahi, Tel Aviv no date). (H)
Kaufmann, Yehezke'el *History of the Jewish Faith* (Bialik and Devir, Tel Aviv, 1972) (4 vols). (H)

Kayyali, Abd al-Wahhab *Palestine: A Modern History* (Al-Muassasa al-Arabiyya lil-Dirasat wa-al-Nashr, Beirut, 1970). (A) All references in the text are to this edition. The book has also been published in an abridged English edition by Croom Helm, London (1978).

Khalidi, Walid (ed.) *From Haven to Conquest: The Palestine Problem until 1949* (Institute for Palestine Studies, Beirut, 1971).

Kluckhohn, Clyde *Mirror for Men: Anthropology and Modern Life* (McGraw-Hill, New York, 1971, (17th printing)).

Lam *War and Education*

Landau, Jacob *The Arabs in Israel* (Ma'arakhot, Israel Ministry of Defence, Tel Aviv, 1971). (H)

—— *The Israeli–Arab Reader* (Bantam Books, New York, 1976, (3rd edn)).

Laqueur, Walter *A History of Zionism* (Schocken Books, New York, 1972).

Lasswell, Harold D.; Leites, Nathan *Language of Politics: Studies in Quantitative Semantics* (Stewart, 1949).

Laws of Israel. Book of Laws No. 37, 1950 (H)

Lehan, Walter "The Jewish National Fund," *Journal of Palestine Studies*, Vol 3, no.4, Summer 1974.

Leiberman, Zvi *In the Mountain of Jerusalem* (Amihai, Tel Aviv, 1953). (H)

Leon, Abram *The Jewish Question: A Marxist Interpretation* (Pathfinder Press, New York, 1972, (2nd printing)).

Lippman, Walter *Public Opinion* (Harcourt Brace, New York, 1922).

Lustick, Ian *Arabs in the Jewish State: Israeli Control of a National Minority* (University of Texas Press, Austin, 1980).

McLellan, David *Marx Before Marxism* (Macmillan, London, 1970).

Margalit, Yossi *Fire in the Woods* (Newman, Tel Aviv, 1959). (H)

Mar'i, Sami *Arab Education in Israel* (Syracuse University Press, Syracuse, 1978).

Mayntz, Renata; Holm, Kurt and Huebner, Roger *Introduction to Empirical Sociology* (Penguin, Harmondsworth, 1976).

Meitiv, Benni *The Sowers in the Desert* (Sifriyat Po'alim, Merhaviyah, 1972). (H)

Mendelsohn, Ezra *Class Struggle in the Pale: The Formative Years of the Jewish Workers Movement in Tsarist Russia* (Cambridge University Press, London, 1970).

Merhav, Peretz *The History of the Workers Movement in the Land of Israel* (Sifriyat Po'alim, Merhaviyah, 1967). (H)

Milstein, Uri *Unit 101*

Mosinson, Yigal *Hasambah in Border Ambushes* (Shalgi Books, Tel Aviv, no date). (H)

—— *Hasambah and the Horse Robbers* (N. Teverski, Tel Aviv, 1951). (H)

—— *Hasambah in Street Fighting in Gaza* (Shalgi Books, Tel Aviv, 1971).

—— *Hasambah in the Cave of Turkelin* (Ramdor, Tel Aviv, 1973). (H)

—— *Hasambah and the Great Secret* (Shalgi Books, Tel Aviv, 1975). (H)

Mu'ammar, Tawfiq *The Memories of a Refugee, or Haifa in the Battle* (Al-Hakim, Nazareth, 1958). (A)

Nadel, Barukh *Neti and the Secret Installation in Acre* (M. Mizrahi, Tel Aviv, 1972). (H)

—— *Neti and the Fearful Events of the Red Rock* (M. Mizrahi, Tel Aviv, 1974). (H)

Nakhleh, Khalil *Palestinian Dilemma: Nationalist Consciousness and University Education in Israel* (Association of American Arab University Graduates, Detroit, 1979).

Naor, Mordechai *The Good Guys Return* (Ma'arakhot, Israel Ministry of Defence, Tel Aviv, 1974). (H)

Newsweek Magazine, 6 February 1969.

New York Times "Israel Bars Rabin from Relating 1948 Eviction of Arabs", 23 October 1979.

Ofek, Uriel *The Paratroopers Are Coming* (Ofer Books, Tel Aviv, 1969a). (H)

—— *Seven Miles and Another Prayer* (J. Chechiq, Tel Aviv, 1969b). (H)

—— *Smoke Covered the Golan* (M.Mizrahi, Tel Aviv, 1974). (H)

Omer, Deborah *The Border Inside the Heart* (J. Sharbarq, Tel Aviv, 1973). (H)

Oren, Barukh *The Adventures of the Heroes* (Am Oved, Tel Aviv, 1964). (H)

Peres "National Education for Arab Youth in Israel: A Comparative Analysis of Curricula", *Jewish Journal of Sociology*

Polk, A. N. "The Origin of the Arabs of the Land of Israel", *Molad,* New Series, Tel Aviv, November 1967. (H)

Qahwaji, Habib *The Arabs under the Israeli Occupation since 1948* (Palestine Research Center, Beirut, 1972). (A)

Rabina, Yirmiyahu *The Story of a Hebrew Guide* (M. Newman, Tel Aviv, 1948). (H)

Robnett, George *Conquest Through Immigration: How Zionism Turned Palestine into a Jewish State* (Institute for Special Research, Pasadena, California, 1968).

Ron-Feder, Galilah *The Three Who Did Not Desert* (Milui, Tel Aviv, 1971). (H)

Ruppin, Arthur *My Life and Work* (Am Oved, Tel Aviv, 1968) (3 vols). (H)

Sadeh, Ezrah *The Last Battle* (Yifat, Jaffa, 1971).

Said, Edward *Orientalism* (Routledge & Kegan Paul, London, 1978).

—— *The Question of Palestine* (Routledge & Kegan Paul, London, 1980)

Salu, Yehudah *Fire in the Mountains* (Am Oved, Tel Aviv, 1970). (H)

Samuel, Beer *Marx and Engels: The Communist Manifesto* (Appleton-Century Crofts, Educational Division, Meredith Corporation, New York, 1955).

Sarig, On *Dannidin in the Service of the Intelligence* (M. Mizrahi, Tel Aviv, 1968a). (H)

—— *Dannidin the Liberator of the Prisoners* (M. Mizrahi, Tel Aviv, 1968b). (H)

—— *Dannidin in the Six Day War* (M. Mizrahi, Tel Aviv, 1977).

Sayigh, Rosemary *Palestinians: From Peasants to Revolutionaries* (Zed Press, London, 1979).

Schwartz, Y. Z. *The War of Independence* (Roubin Mass, Tel Aviv, 1950). (H)

Semoli, Eliezer *Light in the Galilee* (Massadah, Tel Aviv, no date). (H)

—— *The People of the Beginning* (Massadah, Tel Aviv, 1953). (H)

—— *The Sons of the First Rain* (Massadah, Tel Aviv, 1972). (H)

Shaham, Nathan *Now It Is Permitted to Reveal* (Sifriyat Po'alim, Merhaviyah, 1959). (H)

Shahar, David *The Adventures of Ricki Ma'oz* (The Educational and Social Department of the International Zionist Labor Union, Jerusalem, 1961). (H)

Shmueli, Moshe *Zionism and the Labor Movement* (Mifa'lei Tarbut, ve-Hinukh, Tel Aviv, 1961). (H)

Steiner, Zvi *The General Book Catalogue* (PO Box 7303, Jerusalem, updated to August 1975). (H)

Sunday Times, London, 15 June 1969.

Talmi, Eliezer and Menahem, *Zionist Lexicon* (Ma'ariv Books, Tel Aviv, 1977). (H)

Talmi, Emma Levin *Purim in Elul* (Sifriyat Po'alim, Merhaviyah, 1954). (H)

Tamuz, Binyamin *A Boat Sails into the Sea* (Shaharit: A Library for Children and Youth, Jerusalem, no date). (H)

Taylor, Allen *The Zionist Mind* (The Institute for Palestine Studies, Beirut, 1974).

The Jewish Week, "Israeli Youth's Changing Perception of the Arabs", Washington DC, January 1981, pp. 1–7.

Tomeh, George *U.N. Resolutions on Palestine and Israeli Arab Conflict 1947–74* (Institute of Palestine Studies, Beirut, 1978).

Vander, Landen *American Minority Relations: The Sociology of Racial and Ethnic Groups* (Ronold Books, New York, 1966).

Vardi, Zeev *Who Is Running in the Alleys?* (M. Mizrahi, Tel Aviv, 1971). (H)

Waines, David *A Sentence of Exile: The Palestine/Israeli Conflict 1897–1977* (Medina Press, Wilmette, 1977).

Weinberg, Abraham *Few against Many* (Ma'arakhot, Israeli Ministry of Defence, Tel Aviv, 1956).

Weitz, Joseph *My Diary and Letters to the Children* (Massadah, Tel Aviv, 1965) (6 vols). (H)

Wistrich, Robert *Revolutionary Jews from Marx to Trotsky* (George Harrap, London, 1976).

Yefet, Binyamin Zeev *The Password Is Courage* (E. Marcus, Jerusalem, no date). (H)

Zangwill, Israel "The Return to Palestine", *New Liberal Review,* London, December 1901.

Zehavi, Zvi *From ha-Hatam Sofer Until Herzl* (The Zionist Library, Jerusalem, 1967). (H)

Zore'a, Na'omi *Toward the Sand and the Blue Sea* (Ha-Kibbutz ha-Meuhad, 1953). (H)

Zureik, Elia *The Palestinians in Israel: A Study in Internal Colonialism* (Routledge & Kegan Paul, London, 1979).

Appendix

בְּפֶתַח הוֹפִיעַ הַמּוֹרֶה הָעַרְבִי, וּבְיָדוֹ מַגְלֵב בַּעַל רְצוּעוֹת אֲחָדוֹת

The Arab teacher appeared at the door holding in his hand a
multi-striped whip.

Eliezer Semoli, *The Sons of the First Rain*, p. 105.

An Arab on a donkey.
Uriel Ofeq, *Seven Mills and Another Prayer*, p. 25.

A group of Egyptian soldiers listen to stories inside a bunker near the Israeli border.

Yigal Mosinson, *Hasambah and the Great Secret,* pp. 81 & 86.

An Egyptian officer.

Yigal Mosinson, *Hasambah and the Great Secret,* pp. 81 & 86.

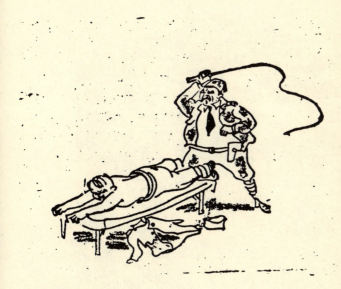

An Egyptian officer lashes with a whip one of his soldiers in order to discover the truth.

Yigal Mosinson, *Hasambah and the Great Secret,* pp. 81 & 86.

מחמוד שלף את חרב ותיפנף בה

Mahmud pulled out his sword and waved it.
Yigal Mosinson, *Hasambah in the caves of Turkelin*, p. 32.

‎— לקום ! — פקד מפקד בית-הכלא

Up! ordered the commander of the prison.
Yigal Mosinson, *Hasambah in Street Fighting in Gaza*, p. 82.

המושל הצבאי ענה והצדיע

] 95 [

The military commander answered (the telephone) and saluted.
Yigal Mosinson, *Hasambah in Street Fighting in Gaza*, p. 95.

142

בְּנִיעַת הָאוֹיֵב

The surrender of the enemy.
On Sarig, *Dannidin in the Six Day War*, p. 81.

הַשֵּׁד כּוֹפִיעַ!

The ghost appears!
On Sarig, *Dannidin in the Intelligence Service*, p. 71.

Azit (the female dog), Gamal Abdul Nasser and General Fuad.
Motah Gur, *Azit in the Palaces of Cairo,* p. 151.

קַבָּלַת פָּנִים לְנָצֶר...

A reception for Nasser . . .
On Sarig, *Dannidin in the Intelligence Service*, p. 81.

‫‫‫-‫אֲנִי מִשְׁתַּתֵּף בְּצַעֲרֶךָ, הַגֶּנֶרָל עַבְּדָלָה...‬

"I share your sorrow, General Abdallah . . ."
On Sarig, *Dannidin the Liberator of the Prisoners*, p. 47.

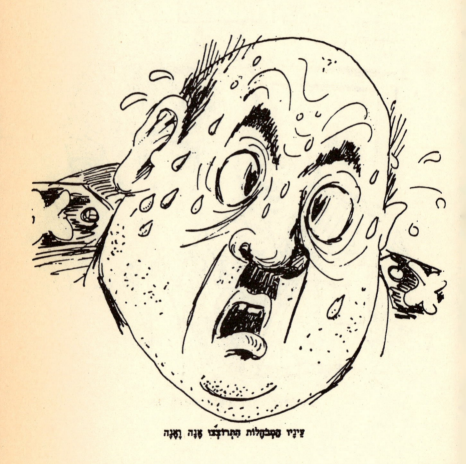

צֵינָיו הַמְבֹהָלוֹת הִתְרוֹצְצוּ אָנֶה וָאָנָה

His frightened eyes ran back and forth (in their sockets).
On Sarig, *Dannidin the Liberator of the Prisoners*, p. 78.

אַחְמָד הוֹצִיא מֶצְבָּטַיִם גְּדוֹלִים

Ahmad took out a large pair of pincers.
On Sarig, *Dannidin the Liberator of Prisoners*, p. 65.